At Home With Work

At Home With Work

*Understanding and Managing Remote
and Hybrid Work*

Nyla Naseer

BEP
BUSINESS EXPERT PRESS
Leader in applied, concise business books

At Home With Work:
Understanding and Managing Remote and Hybrid Work

First published in 2023 by
Business Expert Press, LLC
222 East 46th Street, New York, NY 10017
www.businessexpertpress.com

ISBN-13: 978-1-63742-459-9 (paperback)
ISBN-13: 978-1-63742-460-5 (e-book)

Business Expert Press Human Resource Management and Organizational Behavior Collection

First edition: 2023

10 9 8 7 6 5 4 3 2 1

Description

Remote and hybrid work environments have boomed in number; however, understanding on how to manage remote and hybrid work is still in its infancy. We need better guidance on the impact of remote working on behavior, organizational culture, and well-being, so that remote-working models are optimized for success. *At Home With Work* provides this understanding and guidance.

This book explains the background of remote work: how technology and a changing society created the perfect backdrop to mass adoption of fully remote and hybrid work. It shows how what started as an emergency response to COVID became the biggest global change to working arrangements in living memory and shifted our expectations about work itself.

The author investigates how remote and hybrid work have moved the dynamic away from ego-driven office culture and toward higher trust and collaborative working. This book is a carefully considered overview and introduction to wider changes in the field of work and the global labor market.

At Home With Work investigates how remote and hybrid work has moved the dynamic away from ego-driven office culture and toward higher-trust and collaborative working. It explains how to foster this within different remote working scenarios.

Hybrid and remote work are part of a huge shift in social expectations, job design, and the pricing of work. This book is a carefully considered overview and introduction to wider changes in the field of work and the global labor market.

Keywords

hybrid working; remote working; remote working advantages; remote working disadvantages; working from home; flexible working; great resignation; future of work; four-day week; home office; managing remotely; power dynamics and remote working

Contents

Acknowledgments

Acknowledgment goes to the remote workers, managers, and organizations that spent time discussing with me the pros and cons of remote management, sometimes at a personal level.

I appreciate that it is not easy to talk about how one feels or how we can sometimes feel ill-equipped for change. I hope that this book throws some light onto this new branch of management science.

Introduction

We spend a lot of time working. There is no getting away from the necessity for most people: we have to work. From school, through college, or university, we are coached and guided to fulfill our potential as employees or as people adding economic value, or as business owners or in self-employment. Our jobs define who we are and how we are seen by others. Many people spend at least as much time with their work colleagues as their family members and friends and sometimes much more so. So work is a huge deal, and theories about the way that work is organized and managed are being suggested and tried out all the time.

This book gives workers, managers, and organizations some food for thought about what to consider and how to thrive at work at one of the most exciting and dynamic times in the development of the way that we all work. *At Home With Work* looks at the special circumstances that have driven the explosion in remote and hybrid working: technology and the COVID-19-mandated work from home catalyst. It goes on to look at what makes remote work so appealing, the problems with it, and how to successfully manage it, before taking a flying visit into the future of work in turbulent times.

Remote work is not a passing fad; it is here to stay. According to projections, by 2025, an estimated 70 percent of the workforce will be working remotely at least five days a month in the United States.[1] Globally, remote work is on a rapidly upward trajectory. However, the development of remote work has not been a slow and steady affair: it has burst onto the scene as a result of Covid.

Covid lockdowns enabled the great remote working experiments of 2020/2021 around the world. Sixty percent of the adult working population worked remotely at some point during the first lockdown in the UK, a total of over eight million people or a quarter of the population

---

[1] www.vox.com/recode/2019/10/9/20885699/remote-work-from-anywhere
-change-coworking-office-real-estate.

working remotely, as opposed to half that figure in 2019 according to the UK Office of National Statistics (ONS). As people are no longer required to work from home, this figure has dropped; however, the trend to work at least partly at home continues to rise. Remote work did not disappear at the end of lockdowns. By the spring of 2022, more than a third of working adults in Great Britain still spent at least part of their time working from home.[2]

Remote work came out of the Covid era a stronger force to be reckoned with, silencing its critics in regard to whether it was possible to transfer work to remote settings, at scale and across industries. Instead of the feared loss of productivity through people "shirking at home," the productivity of many people actually increased when they worked remotely. When the dangers presented by Covid subsided and people could once more return to their offices and other premises, there was an abject sitting on hands and reluctance to give up the new found flexibility. Having assumed that it would be back to business as usual after the pandemic passed, some corporate executives were perplexed; people just did not return dutifully to the office in the way that they had projected. They insisted on staying home. We are now at a place where the new reality of changed expectations and work norms is colliding into long-held and heavily invested-into beliefs about organizational culture, power relationships, and management practices.

Remote and hybrid working looks to be a large and permanent sector of how work is offered, both now and in the future. It makes sense. At a time when more and more work functions can be undertaken from any location using technology, why not capitalize on the efficiencies that this way of working brings? When people value work flexibility over pay, organizations cannot afford to ignore the clarion call of a new era in work organization. Ignoring the expectations of a labor force that has relative ease in moving to alterative employment elsewhere is bad for business.

So there is now a scramble to work out what to do for the best. What "mix" of remote compared to on-site working arrangements should organizations adopt? Should there be one model or should there be different

---

[2] www.ons.gov.uk/employmentandlabourmarket/peopleinwork/employmentandemployeetypes/articles/ishybridworkingheretostay/2022-05-23.

variations to suit different groups of employees? How can organizational culture be maintained or established when most people are working in a hybrid or remote way? Practically, how should managers actually manage their teams in a hybrid/remote world of work? Given the speed with which remote work has become a key part of how we work, it is not surprising that many of these questions are just starting to be asked, let alone answered. *At Home With Work* asks these questions and considers the practical options.

The upheaval offers great opportunity but also holds considerable risk. The challenge is to find solutions and options that don't just mirror the accepted truths that have been applied before, but which may no longer be fit for purpose. We need to go back to first principles and look at how people actually think and behave as workers, but also as people with lives, priorities, and expectations that may be uncomfortably out of sync with the conventional respected thinking about work. Failing to appreciate how power relationships have been completely altered, even subverted by the experience of remote work during Covid lockdowns, and hybrid work postlockdown, will be a mistake. The change in power relationships should be viewed at a catalyst for better work and a different and more effective way of managing.

The question is not just "should work be remote or on-site?" The issue is also one of examining how our behavior is affected by working increasingly online and how to design work to take account of this. Remote work, though popular, does have its potential downsides: isolation and loneliness, communication problems, and burnout, for example. Working out how to manage purely remote or a hybrid model of work that includes both remote and face-to-face work will involve thinking about how the potentially harmful or inefficient outcomes of remote work can be mitigated. People have different personalities and ways of working and therefore will respond in different ways to new ways of working. Ignoring issues will lead to potentially very negative outcomes for individuals and organizations and cause the conundrum of a working population wanting to work flexibly but being increasingly dissatisfied by their experience of it alongside organizations feeling increasingly aware that they are not managing hybrid and remote working well.

Other perceived problems are more nuanced than they at first appear. For example, current advancement of new recruits very much depends on learning from more experienced hands, and this is seen to be more difficult when people work remotely. This could be a real problem or it could be manufactured problem that is more about maintaining a status quo which has benefited leaders and managers in the past. Hybrid and remote working involves adjustment for organizations, workers, and managers, and this book walks you through some of the ways to combat problems and create a successful, productive, and enjoyable working environment and experience. One thing is for sure, business as usual is not an option.

The vast majority of workers in the UK and in other major economies now say that they want the flexibility to continue to at least partly work from home (84 percent in the UK according to ONS figures in 2022). Despite the UK Government immediately after the end of Covid lockdowns pressing organizations to encourage staff to return to offices, many organizations, especially in professional sectors, have acknowledged that they won't be able to attract the best staff unless they offer at least hybrid working.

These are dramatic changes in an almost unbelievably short period of time. How on earth has this been possible? The journey to mainstreaming remote and hybrid working has been underpinned by some fundamental changes in society. Although Covid has been the catalyst, the move toward remote work started a long time ago. Indeed, the debate about whether work should be more accessible and flexible has always been around. Any discussion of where we are now cannot omit how technology has enabled the seismic shift in what we can do remotely and how our expectations have changed in parallel.

COVID-19 provided the practical experience that cemented our expectations of remote work, while providing the important points for reflection from which we can completely rethink our approach to where and how we work. Importantly, it also proved the technology, without which modern remote work would not be possible.

Background

Technology Made Remote Work Possible

The catalyst behind where we currently work (i.e., either in a physical office, remotely, or some mixture of these) has been Covid. However, the ability to have a remote or hybrid option for work is technology-based: without the ability to be online, there would be no remote work.

Let us look at the revolution in technology over the past 10 years and understand how technology has brought about the ability to undertake work from home and has also changed the way that people think and behave at work and elsewhere.

Even before Covid, work was already almost unrecognizably different to what we did in similar roles at the start of the millennium. The changes have been accelerated by many global events but are underpinned by one thing: technology. It is technology that has enabled us to move from an essentially local existence to one that is interrelated on a daily basis with everyone else on earth. Technology has progressively impacted upon, and then controlled every aspect of our lives and simultaneously liberates and constrains us. I'll now look at how technology has enabled remote working and why we need to think about its limitations and impact on our behavior and well-being as part of our overall work design strategy, be this remote, hybrid, or on-site.

At its best, technology enables human development as well as economic growth. It plays a part in reducing poverty, increasing the standard of living, bolstering educational attainment, and improving health. It can contribute to building democratic societies marked by involvement, participation, and transparency. The use of technology in driving forward improvements in the medical, sustainable energy, and environmental fields is truly incredible. These changes are heralding new positive, revolutionary phases of development in these fields.

Cloud computing, the Internet of Things, and Big Data will connect us superefficiently and make everything available digitally everywhere. 5G will bring a new level to connectivity and technologies not even imagined yet will accelerate what is possible beyond our current comprehension.

Technology allows us to talk through a screen in a multitude of ways: text, message, social media (video, message, and call), encrypted message, and even virtual reality. It enables us to pay for things using our phone. It allows us to order products and have them delivered to our door with very little delay or order transport that turns up anywhere at any time. We can play games with any number of people located anywhere on earth online. We can talk to a virtual assistant like Alexa and control other devices using it. At work, we can plan, measure, analyze, and control things and information, and that's just scratching the surface. Technology offers us a world of possibilities that not only make remote work possible but also creates a lifestyle that depends on technological connection. Technology has transformed the way that transactions are conducted, health care happens, training is delivered, factories operate, transport works, and everything else.

The huge impact of one area of technology is particularly relevant to creating the conditions needed for a massive global shift to remote work: communication. I'm not just referring to the existence of tools to enable real-time work communications; I am talking about the place of communication as a driver of expectation. Without communications technology that allows opinions to be shared and people to identify with others who think as they do, the kind of support needed to embed remote working as a cultural norm might not have been possible.

The use of technology means that people can be remotely connected at work. Online communication provides us all with the potential to learn new skills and has opened up collaboration like never before. It is this that has ultimately permitted a, albeit crude, replacement for talking face-to-face with people via the use of messaging tools such as Teams and Zoom, more "formal" descendants of social media.

Although digital technology brings many improvements, it also has many undesirable features including the potential to exploit, mislead, and dumb-down at a societal level. It spawns other problems such as providing constant digital distractions which can become addictive, digital narcissism, and the use of information as a weapon. As we develop a more sophisticated remote work strategy, we need to consider how to minimize and deal with these "dark-side" issues. Communicating remotely (even by video) changes the communication skills that we acquire. The pace that we work at online can have a profound impact on how we think and behave, both as individuals and as a society. By understanding how people behave, we can design the most optimum technology-accessed work.

The Internet has enabled anyone with unrestricted access to view the same information. Information exchange lets people collaborate across teams, departments, organizations, and even more widely in the online public domain. This "democratizing" of information must be juxtaposed against some negatives such losing control of our own information and security concerns. Working remotely means that we exchange more information than ever before, posing a very high risk to our privacy and potential exploitation of our information. This risk is recognized; governments and organizations are making real efforts to ensure that the online world is potentially regulated and secured in order to minimize harm. Legislation such as the General Data Protection Regulation (GDPR) is starting to address issues of information ownership in a more formal way. However, much online security is essentially down to everyone taking personal responsibility for their own data and therefore carries significant risks—risks that are multiplied when we work remotely online.

We are now conditioned to live according to the rhythm of the web and we not only expect but we demand that it helps us out. Changes to our behavior as a result of working online are likely to be exaggerated as we undertake more remote work. We have become used to things being tailored for us, from suggestions for friends to what we might like to buy. This algorithm-driven "autosuggest" mentality has a big presence at work in workflow apps and in a vast range of functions, from marketing and business development to health care and engineering. The expectation that we are walked through a process is now hardwired into our psyche. Increasingly, we are shown exactly what we need to do to succeed toward a particular goal and where we sit in relation to our peers in terms of progress toward that goal. This should make reaching goals a lot easier: workflow is shortened and the challenge of thinking what to do next is reduced. This has obvious benefits for work since we are basically told what to do next—but could this create some problems also?

Whereas we used to have to physically do stuff and work out what to do next, we now often have no contact with, or even knowledge of, automated stages. Making things very easy has some negative repercussions, including boredom and de-skilling. Take using sat-nav instead of relying on a map: the old-fashioned challenge of navigating and undertaking spatial tasks actually keeps our brains alert and may even ward off age-related degeneration.

Life is about challenge. By having much of the "hard work" taken away from us, we also lose the control we have in deciding options for ourselves and the challenge that we need to have a satisfying life. Having things easy does not always make us much happy or lead to better outcomes. Remote work needs to be engineered in a way that replaces the challenge that has taken away some of the quality of experience from work.

So, working online makes things easier but it could also de-skill us. The ultimate de-skilling could be the reduction in our ability to maintain "real" human relationships and interactions. Can workers, increasingly tied to the screen rather than physically present, fully develop the complex skills and judgment needed for satisfying "in-person" relationships?

Our relationships when working with colleagues online are not immune from the same issues that affect us in terms of online communication generally: miscommunication and even online bullying. On the other hand, communicating online gives us potentially greater flexibility in terms of who we engage with, and this could be very positive in terms of both work performance and avoiding the stress of working alongside people we don't necessarily get on with. Ultimately, work entails being with a diverse range of people, including those we might not get on with eye-to-eye. Building tolerance is an important aspect of the remote/hybrid debate about work and its management.

Creativity has a massive home online; the freedom to express oneself to huge number of others is unparalleled in history. Creativity is a key element in work across industries, not just the "creative" industries, and it is important for tasks that involve problem-solving. What impact does working online and remotely have on creativity when compared to interacting more face-to-face? There is no straightforward answer. It is possible to draw inspiration from a whole world of information online. On the other hand, divergent thinking (the free-flowing, creative way that we think) is enhanced by engaging face-to-face with others and even by moving around—two conditions that are generally absent when working through a screen.

What does moving our working routine online do to our well-being, especially since the concern is growing about the wider lifestyle and well-being implications of spending too much time online? Presumably, work is less addictive for most people than social media (although there may be some exceptions), but the potential to work relentlessly in an "always-on" way is still a risk to health and well-being. A hyperconnected environment means that work is there for us to access all the time. For some people, the opportunity leads to obligation and burnout.

We are all easily fooled into confusing the ability to have lots of tabs open showing that we are "multitasking" with actually being more productive. We are not. We can only concentrate on one thing at a time, and for your brain, these things do not even have to be cerebral: simply walking or looking at something also requires processing power—try walking and typing a message into your phone and you will see what I mean. Switching tabs needs a lot of brain power to recover memory attached to each task and is therefore very wasteful, not to mention tiring. It is far better to do one task at a time with your full attention.

More fundamentally, a life glued to screens, whatever the reason, is likely to make us more physically unhealthy, most obviously because we are not going to be moving around an office or other workplace if we are working from a desk at home. We can move around of course, but this will depend on motivating ourselves to do so. Considering that some of us had trouble motivating ourselves to change out of our pyjamas during lockdown, the motivation to exercise when remote-working long-term might prove elusive.

These are just a few of the issues that have developed as a consequence of an increasingly technologically led online work environment for a great number of people. They impact on the basic ways in which we are hard-wired to behave in terms of some very basic and primitive attributes such as communication, motivation, and concentration. Technology provided the tools and change in the nature of work that was a precursor to remote and hybrid working, but it has also changed our behavior, and this needs to be taken into account when designing how work is arranged and how remote and hybrid works are managed.

Technology enabled jobs to change fundamentally. Online working has created the potential for many people to work at any time and from anywhere. However, even with this potential, before 2020, people by and large worked for a set working week with set hours and at a set location that they traveled to from their home. Then, COVID-19 happened. Virtually overnight, people were compelled to work from home, signaling a massive, global seismic reinterpretation of how and where work was undertaken by the billions of people working in offices worldwide. The pandemic was long-lasting enough to create a genuine shift in behavior, create new habits, and ultimately create a new set of expectations about work. This did not just relate to where work was conducted but also the very nature of work itself.

Covid: The Big Remote-Work Experiment

A time traveler dialing into mid-2022 from a few years earlier would not believe that their time machine was functioning normally. After all, when they left, people were spending more or less the same time period at work premises as they had done previously in their working lives, undertaking the same sort of commute and negotiating the same sort of working relationships that they had done in the past. The world where they exist, the post-Covid world, might appear the same for a few hours as they walk down a street: the same houses, shops, and offices, and people going about their daily lives seemingly as normal. Start spending a bit more time and asking a few questions, and the differences start emerging. The world has changed. Quite apart from the battered, Covid-related notices are still in evidence in public buildings and spaces, and there are other, more fundamental changes.

Many people across vast swathes of the economy no longer travel to work in regular offices any more. Many sectors now operate on a hybrid basis, expecting staff to work partly from home and partly from the office. Within these sectors, there are some organizations that have gone further: allowing workers to work from home on a permanent basis so eliminating the need to commute, work face-to-face with others, or stick to specific timings for work.

The economy is not impacted evenly by these changes. At first sight, some industries where there is no option but to go to a place of work and work alongside others appear pretty much untouched by the changes: warehousing, retail, factory work, and services such as medical care or hairdressing. Yet, scratch beneath the surface and in these sectors too, there are changes, some due to Covid realignment and some due to other, more structural changes that have been emerging over many years because of the growth of technology, globalization, and shifts in expectation about work and society. In these sectors, administrative functions such as finance or marketing are conducted on a remote basis, while people working in other sections continue to go into work premises.

In other sectors, Covid has accelerated changes to the work environment and the very nature of work that were already germinating and growing. So for office jobs that were mainly carried out on a computer, the opportunity to work from home became at first a legal obligation and then an option offered by some organizations and a permanent change for others.

The work-from-home revolution has been concentrated in those areas where people can work via a computer. Technology had just about got there with the option for people to talk freely and easily online, and work process apps and programs for almost any function needed were available when the Covid pandemic struck. The availability of cloud computing has made a reality of the transfer of mind-blowing amounts of information and computational activity. So, activities like back-office functions, already on their way to automation, became even more so and many of us beavered away on freshly delivered laptops in our home-office or spare bedroom. If you have worked in administration of any sort, a desk at a corporate office swapped for a desk in your own home made sense to most people. After all, 70 to 90 percent of your work-time was probably spent on-screen within your old physical office, and the rest was the "nonessential" (even inefficient) time spent chatting to others, often about nonwork-related stuff. Even this chit-chat could be replaced by the online version of water-cooler conversation (WhatsApp or Teams chat), so, on the face of it, a win-win outcome given the extraordinary times we went through.

It was not just specific functions that went from office-based to work-from-home. During Covid times, if you could work from home, you had to. This meant that huge parts of the economy where people did not solely work at a computer, but also interacted with other people in some form or another, also had work redesigned so that they could work from home. So people who served customers in banks now arranged online appointments, teachers conducted online lessons, and personal trainers offered online routines. GPs no longer saw patients in the surgery, instead offering telephone consultations; initially, a short-term change for obvious reasons given the need to protect patients, this policy had massive public support. However, several years later, GPs still remain online or on a phone for most people, leading some people to think that the days of face-to-face GP consultations for all are being confined to history (at least in the UK). This also seems to hold true for other professional groups, including many local authority professionals who, years after the Covid pandemic, still largely work from home.

Other professions, not wanting to miss out and inspired by the remote-working opportunities highlighted during Covid, are keenly trying to find ways to conduct their work online and turning to tech to make it so. So, architects are now viewing projects virtually, actors are now offering virtual performance, and counselors have switched from personal to online consultations. As people work increasingly remotely themselves, it may be that we all become accepting of the online delivery of virtually any service, including those that we may never have previously felt could be undertaken remotely.

During the Covid era, there were obvious constraints on home-working. For a start, if you had to be "in-situ" such as somewhere where you had to have access to immobile equipment or facilities, such as a factory or hospital, you could not work remotely. Physically handling stock also ruled out remote working and jobs where you offered a person-to-person service such as hairdressing or massage were not easily translatable into a remote format (however, online instruction enabling people to DIY almost anything became very, very popular over lockdown).

From the start, there was a divide between groups of people and professions that had options to work remotely or not. People not able to work at home had to go to their regular premises (or were furloughed), but overall, it tended to be white-collar workers who worked remotely. This group included higher earning professionals and lower earning administrative workers. Interestingly, over time, the facility to work at home has been retained for more senior staff but has sometimes been rescinded for those nearer the bottom of the ladder. Professional jobs that tend to pay well, such as general practice medicine, even if appearing not that amenable to remote working, have switched the majority of their work to being remote. Meanwhile, frontline workers have stayed in-person. Overall, there are plenty of middle-status technical and administrative jobs where the opportunity to negotiate (or demand) hybrid or remote working is now on the cards and where the next few years will reveal just how embedded this new aspect of work will become. To most people, it looks very likely to become a permanent feature of work for demographic and cultural reasons.

Since the start of the remote-working era (postlockdown), it is mid-career workers aged 30 to 49 who have been most likely to work in a hybrid way and younger workers (16 to 29) who are most likely to work entirely from home across age groups.[1] In my view, the "normality" of remote working for younger age groups will translate into greater proportions of people in the entire working population taking up hybrid, if not fully remote working, within the next decade.

Alongside the many different combinations of work-setup now available in the post-Covid world, there is also, by necessity, a whole industry that has grown to service the new work-from-home environment, be this remote-working hardware and software or the massive expansion of almost instant (well, within an hour) home delivery services of anything from groceries to flowers and kits to make everything from meals to crafts. Fortuitously, the technology that enables these services to be ordered, bought, paid for, and delivered had just about matured in time for the great remote-working revolution. People even acquired more pets to keep them company as they worked from home and were able to have individually designed pet food bought by online subscription and delivered to their door.

Other clues point to permanent changes in the priorities and thinking of people with changed values. During Covid, there was torrid interest in moving away from cities and into the countryside, away from the stress (and potentially higher infection rates) of urban areas. With the ability to work from home becoming a permanent choice in people's minds, they no longer felt constrained to live within a commuting radius. People were seeking a different way of life; one that reflected a certain new found freedom and a change in expectations of what they wanted from life and work and what they were prepared to compromise for work. This structural change process accelerated because of Covid, but it did not

---

[1] www.ons.gov.uk/employmentandlabourmarket/peopleinwork/employmentandemployeetypes/articles/ishybridworkingheretostay/2022-05-23.

start with Covid and it will not end with it either; it is an ongoing and evolutionary global shift.

The shift has also been made possible by a change in the way that people (especially younger generations of employees) see themselves in relation to work. Their expectations have changed along with the development of sense of entitlement that has been growing for the past few decades. This, coupled with new self-belief systems such as "manifestation" of desired outcomes, means that once people feel entitled to work remotely, it has become very difficult to break the belief that people are entitled to work in at least a hybrid setup. Erosion of the old culture of deference to one's employer, together with new found confidence to be assertive, has tipped the balance of expectation away from what employers want and toward what employees and prospective employees want.

Hybrid and remote working are smart for organizations. There are massive efficiencies to be gained from the removal of the need for physical office space (often the biggest cost to a business after wages) and the ability to hire the best people wherever they live, even abroad. Organizations can deliver information and training to large number of people unconstrained by room capacity. People can work flexibly more easily, thus enabling parents and careers to work when they may have previously been unable to. People can have a greater sense of well-being that comes with greater autonomy over their work.

Another very significant factor feeding into where people want or are prepared to work and one that directly relates to Covid itself is the fear of infection from Covid or any other yet unknown pathogen. Different groups of people have understandably reacted very differently to the end of lockdown and the opening up of society (including the expectation that people return to working on-site). Some people, especially those who have personally been unwell with Covid, are in high-risk groups or have loved ones who have suffered, and are much more cautious about returning to an office where people are working in close proximity. It is irrelevant whether the actual risk that people face is real, as fear alone can make working away from home almost impossible for people with the belief that they are at high risk of being infected at work. As each new virus or infectious disease reaches the headlines, the fear of going back into a work office grows.

It was initially assumed during lockdown that people would avoid working as much as possible when expected to do this remotely, leading to the phrase "shirking at home." However, this was debunked as the vast majority of employers reported that remote staff productivity was at least up to the same level as when people went into the office and sometimes exceeded it. Possible explanations included more concentrated periods of work as people did not have colleagues to chat to, a removal of self-sabotage to keep in line with others' lower productivity, and a feeling that it was a duty to work hard, given the trust put in people working remotely. Some people may also have worked tirelessly without the normal cues given by being in a group environment and with the constant online availability of work to do, seemingly unable to switch off.

The level of success of remote work amid all the turmoil of Covid was something of a surprise. People worked hard, often in the absence of any effective management. They stayed engaged with their colleagues and took the opportunity to upskill. Of course, the level of commitment was probably related in part to the feeling that not working effectively could put people on a fast track to being fired but, nevertheless, people did far more than the bare minimum. People in the entire workforce developed (either first- or second-hand) experience of working in a way that was more flexible than many could have ever previously imagined. The floodgates of expectation had been opened, and this was the real turning point for some type of remote working to become the norm rather than an aberration.

After lockdown, people in many organizations had assumed that complete remote working was going to continue in the long term. Some had even relocated as they thought they would never have to commute again. Unfortunately, for these "remote-first" preference holders, most companies, even tech companies such as Apple and Google, went with a hybrid model of work rather than totally remote. Many CEOs wrote strongly worded opinion pieces on the desirability of being physically present in the office. David Solomon, Goldman Sachs CEO, called remote working an "aberration" that was not possible to sustain long term because of issues such as appropriately inducting new workers and ensuring their career development. Other global banking and finance CEOs expressed similar views. In June 2021, Tim Cook, Apple CEO, sent out a memo, sharing an expectation that employees would return to working in-office from later that year. The staff pushed back, saying that there was a lack of realism in what the executive was saying, given the changed lives of people who had more than proved their productivity while working in a remote environment. Apple now offers a hybrid working model; Tim Cook having acknowledged by September 2021 that Apple would not return to totally in-office working because, as he said: "We've found that there are some things that actually work really well virtually."[2]

Workers understandably reacted negatively to what they saw as veiled or direct threats to their employment or conditions if they did not return to the office. Some firms mandated some degree of in-office working, while others suggested a pay reduction for workers who want to continue working from home. With some businesses holding their cards very close to their chest when it comes to individual salary agreements, it is possible that firms are already discounting pay rewards by significant amounts for people who want to work totally remotely, or outside the scope of the company's "normal" working arrangements. Companies are rumored to be cutting salaries by up to 25 percent for a totally remote option.

Perhaps, this is not entirely out of line with what employees have said that they would bear in order to keep working remotely. An American Goodhire study found that, out of lockdown, 61 percent of respondents said that they would be willing to take a pay cut to continue working remotely, with some people willing to take a cut of up to 50 percent. The survey results showed the lengths that people said that they would be willing to go to in order to stay working remotely, with a quarter of people saying that they would quit straight away if told they had to return to on-site full-time and 70 percent saying that they would be willing to sacrifice other benefits including company pensions.[3] So business pay cuts for the privilege of remote working may be the start of a recalibration of how work is valued.

A few large firms have insisted on total on-site working (including Netflix and Goldman Sachs at time of writing) and some have gone

[2] www.imore.com/tim-cook-admits-apples-remote-work-policy-could-change.
[3] www.goodhire.com/resources/articles/state-of-remote-work-survey/.

"remote-first," including Deloitte. The vast majority, however, have settled on a hybrid model for people for whom working remotely was undertaken during the pandemic. Perhaps, scared by the idea of a "Great Resignation" with surveys in 2021 (near to the end of lockdowns) signaling how many people would walk out of their current jobs if remote working ended completely, many organizations instead offered the pragmatic solution of hybrid-working.

Work in a Changing Society

Latent demand for permanent flexible working, including remote working, has been unlocked by the Covid pandemic. However, the demand for more flexibility is in line with bigger changes in the way that people think and the inevitable pressures this brings to work practices that, by standing still, move further and further away from effective and efficient ways of operating.

Work has been changed by technology and globalization, and people have been changed alongside this. Wider changes in society have been accelerated by social media, and these have then led to changes to expectations about work in the past few decades. The Covid pandemic then threw a curveball into the whole picture and turbocharged moves like remote working and concern for emotional well-being. So, what exactly are some of these big changes?

Since 1970s, there has been a gradual decline in "production sector" employment. Employment in mining and quarrying, manufacturing, and utilities fell by 65 percent between 1970 and 2016 in the UK. The UK has shifted to being a service sector economy with about 80 percent of people now working in this sector. In particular, scientific and technical services employment has nearly tripled in the period. These structural changes in employment have paved the way for remote working: jobs have disappeared from industries which cannot be undertaken remotely (like coal-mining and manufacturing) and have been created in existing and new sectors where work is more suited to a remote work environment (like education or communications services).[1] Without the underlying changes in the types of jobs we do, the whole remote-working conversation would not be happening.

So, a lot of people have been working in jobs that theoretically could be undertaken remotely, but, until Covid, people still went into

---

[1] www.ons.gov.uk/economy/economicoutputandproductivity/output/articles /changesintheeconomysincethe1970s/2019-09-02.

workplaces to do them. As work changed, so the people doing it changed also. The "de-masculinization" of work in terms of the rapid disappearance of heavy industry was accompanied by a switch into an increasingly important services sector with a strong office culture where power hierarchies thrived and managers were seen as the lynchpins of the organization. Offices provide perfect environments for "command and control" management where people can be personally graded on the way that they fit in with the norms of behavior. These environments have tended to reward people who are in sync with those holding the most power around the office—generally the managers. Within these workplaces, qualities like being confident and liked by top people often lead to higher approval and potentially career advancement without the appreciation that this could be unfair. So, for many years, working in an office has meant adjusting to the inevitable office politics that accompanies it.

Organizational culture is a huge discipline of course, and many efforts have been made to eliminate cultures which can stifle talent and potential. However, most of us have experienced workplaces where, even if well-intentioned, the culture is still based on who fits in with a strongly monopersonality-based hierarchy.

Other things have been changing. Work has become increasingly global and more people are directly working with international colleagues or at the very least appreciate the way that their business is dependent on global supply chains of goods or labor. Around us in our communities, we live in diverse communities with differences of opinion and culture. Alongside this diversity, a series of revised expectations about work are starting to become universally accepted, with people increasingly likely to move their labor to employers who match their expectations most closely.

The rise of social media has enabled the very rapid discussion, reaction to and adoption of ideas in a way that has not been possible in any previous era. It is particularly successful in taking experiences and translating them into givens of what should or shouldn't happen. So, whereas in the past, accepted codes of behavior were only changed slowly (often over successive generations as people refined their ideas from their youth thought to middle-aged thought); change in expectations is now more rapid. Social media, especially platforms like Instagram, have enabled people to imagine lives that are time-rich and trouble-free. The portrayal of lifestyles that offer a vision that is very different to the reality of most people working in regular jobs is influencing the thinking of people who are influenced by social media—and that's a huge number of people.

The trend for people to state that their dream job is to be a "social media influencer," working from anywhere in the world (glamorous locations preferred) and with plenty of cash and friends, has become a real thing. In fact, back in 2019, a study found that one in five British children between 11 and 16 stated that they wanted a career as a social media influencer.[2] Of course, most people's lives are not and will not be similar to what is portrayed on social media. The lives of social media influencers are not even like the image portrayed on their own channels. What is important is that people start to feel entitled to something equating to what they see on social media.

Some of the key changes in expectation promoted by social media have been around what is "fair" and not. The aftermath of the financial crash brought with it winners and losers: the winners being those with assets and the losers being younger people unlikely to be able to afford the traditional "rites of passage" assets such as a home of their own. Logically and very practically people switched to valuing experiences rather than measuring their success purely against owning assets (while also trying new ways to get the assets they still wanted). This way of thinking solidly supports increased flexibility as a key work aspiration. In place of the higher salaries and assets that many people know are not immediately achievable, they can insist on enhancing their lives by giving themselves the freedom and flexibility to use their time in the way that they want and be in the places they want to be.

This does not mean of course that people are not interested in money, they are, but as a sort of psychological self-esteem protection mechanism, we can all pragmatically change our priorities so that we are focused on achievable goals. For a generation of people for whom ever owning a property may be unrealistic, having more control over the working environment and schedule is a way to have tangible control over life.

---

[2] www.hrreview.co.uk/hr-news/1-of-5-british-children-want-a-career-as-social-media-influencers/.

It is not a case of fooling yourself. Just owning stuff is genuinely not the secret to happiness, especially when compared to spending quality time doing things we enjoy with people whose company we value. What has changed is that social media is now full of influencers and messages telling people about the importance of having experiences and freedom, although curiously this is often interwoven with the need to buy products as part of the new flexible lifestyle portrayed. New industries have popped up, portraying themselves as integral to the new flexible lifestyles that are emerging. In particular, app-based delivery of everything from takeaway food to laundry have focused their business strategy on the idea that people need to have access to home delivery if they are working from home.

Since people still want (and feel entitled to) the big ticket items that money can buy, some people have also turned to technology to try and fill the gap. "Financial Freedom" has become a buzz work online. A large number of people (mainly younger people) invest in share and asset trading via their mobiles and many have embraced the "side-gig" culture, doing everything from delivering takeaways to online tutoring. These "hustle-based" lifestyles need flexibility to operate, not the nine to five. Alongside remote working, this is perhaps the biggest innovation in work styles, whether through necessity or choice, people are earning money through a mix of jobs, self-employment, and self-designed investment plans (many of which are essentially gambling). Go back a few years and such a mix of activities would have been very difficult but as technology has provided the tools and people have provided the desire to take risks and try different strategies, hustle-based lives are a reality for growing numbers. The more flexible employed-work becomes, the more opportunity exists for adding income by doing another activity. What used to be called "moonlighting" has been brought up to date and looks as if it is her to stay. Indeed, people who work this way sometimes prefer the variety and freedom of opportunity that it affords.

Not everyone who embraces more flexible working does so in order to have a side-gig of course, at least not a paying one. Many people just want to structure their time so that it fits in with their life, whether this is because of other obligations or other priorities that they have chosen for themselves. Older people in particular may be fortunate in not needing flexibility to earn money elsewhere; they may just want the time to pursue other personal interests. People in high-earning roles may decide that they would rather earn less and work less hours than work full time. For example, in 2021, the Royal College of Physicians said that a fifth of doctors already worked part-time hours and the majority of trainee doctors entering the NHS said that they were interested in working part time. So it seems that everyone wants flexibility: those who need extra money and those who are happy to sacrifice some money for more time.

A popular reason to sacrifice money for time is to spend time with family. This matters even more if people are bringing up children. The "you can't relive childhood" mantra is a very strong argument for flexible working. Even if you don't have children, you still "only live once," so being able to live in your dream location, for example, is a far bigger deal than in the past.

Many issues have been popularized via social media and have made an impact that affects people's thoughts about life and work. Justice movements like Black Lives Matter and Me Too have a tangible and lasting impact on the aspirations and values of people and can strongly influence how organizations want to portray themselves if only because they want to appear progressive and in the vanguard of positive change. For employees, policies like remote working may be rolled up with supporting progress in general. Allowing workers to work remotely could be interpreted as a sign that an employer wants staff members to be "themselves" and empathizes with their desire for more freedom to live and work in the way that suits them.

There is another major social factor that is highly relevant to the debate about the way that work is conducted. It is an issue that influences people in the UK and globally: that of the state of people's mental health. Mental well-being among young people in particular has been declining for some years globally as a result of a variety of reasons including worsening economic prospects, the impact and insecurities caused by social media, and uncertainty about the future, centered around concerns about climate change and the effect on the planet. The COVID-19 pandemic prompted a new level of mental ill health which was coupled with long delays in accessing medical care. In the United States, a survey for the Centers for Disease Control and Prevention suggested that almost two-thirds of 18- to 24-year olds reported symptoms of anxiety or depression during the pandemic.[3] On top of the uncertainty that was already facing young people, the impact of Covid at a time when they envisaged making new connections and building a base for later life was a severe blow. Because mental ill health at a young age can lead to persistent ill health, this is a real cause for concern.

We are at a place where anxiety appears to be almost endemic in many people's lives, especially if you happen to be young. This is sobering but if there is one silver lining it is that people seem to have embraced the importance of well-being as an important factor in their lives. They now also hold expectations that employers will priorities well-being for their staff. Social media enables people to share their concerns about mental health, without associating it with shame as used to be the case. This helps people feel emboldened about making decisions to protect their own mental health and well-being. Since the work environment is a key source of stress for a great many people, it is easy to see how employees highly value having the flexibility to work in ways that they feel will reduce any negative impacts they associate with work, be this the commute to work, working in close proximity with people that cause them stress, or just having time and space to practice self-care at home.

Concurrently, organizations are taking their positions in terms of their stance. Of course, the emphasis is on improving and supporting employee well-being, as well as meeting the strategic need to operate in an effective way and respond to the realities of a changing labor market where people are not so willing to work 100 percent on-site compared to the past. At present, this seems to be very much led by the feelings held by senior leaders (most often the CEO or founder) on where people should work, rather than by any analytical process, although I feel sure that there will be much more scientific interrogation of what model works best in individual scenarios.

---

[3] www.nytimes.com/2020/08/24/well/family/young-adults-mental-health -pandemic.html.

Changed Expectations About Work

Our childhood expectation is that we will enjoy work. We start off life full of hope. Ask a child what they want to do when they grow up, and they will name or describe their dream job with wide eyes and excitement. For kids, their intended favorite job should be an adventure, a source of joy and self-respect, something that makes them happy, somewhere where they are to do interesting things with interesting people. For a child, what they want to do for a job reflects their own likes and ability, and a future workplace is mostly imagined as stable and stress-free. You can see kids playing together in helpful ways, being great team members and having great success fixing problems from mending people who are "broken" to building feats of engineering. In a child's world, work itself is an adventure that they control and develop, adjusting to new challenges and suggestions from playmates in ways that put professional business strategists to shame.

Of course, a child should not be thinking about the complexities of working relationships, office politics, the necessity of boring and often mundane work as part of the mix, or feeling trapped/deskilled/overlooked, or the many other potential concerns we have as adults at work. That is not to say that real work should be some sort of fairytale, indeed developing a realistic approach to work and developing a resilience when faced with work we would rather not do, or problems that we find difficult to work out, is an important part of developing maturity in relation to work. However, there is no getting away from the fact that many people progressively find the reality of work to be a big disappointment. Indeed, discontent at work can lead to major problems both for workers and organizations if not handled effectively.

Organizations do not refer back to childhood dreams. They tend to focus on issues of returns, productivity, and performance. They operate in competitive markets both for customers and for retaining the best staff.

All sorts of risks stalk business and organizations, from changes in leg-islation to bad press, to macroeconomic circumstances, and even major unforeseen disruption as we saw with the COVID-19 pandemic. Workers also have to deal with how changes in the broader economy impact on their finances and level of security and have to adjust to changes in their personal lives and thinking that may impact on their work.

People are influenced by what goes on around them, what they perceive the status quo to be, and, increasingly, where they feel that they fit in terms of society and identity. Our feelings about these issues create expectations about our lives and work. If you were transported back in time to an era when people had far fewer rights, for example to a feudal society, you would probably feel uncomfortable and find it difficult to adjust. Once you have expectations, it is very difficult to accept a less-good deal (one reason why some people in the past have struggled with moving "sideways" at work). People inherently think that *they* are right and when we meet other people that think the same way as us this reinforces our views. The ease with which we can now have our attitudes reinforced by large numbers of people online is a major reason why attitudes to work have changed so dramatically over the past few years—without us even realizing.

In the past, when society tended to be more compliant, we more readily accepted the things we did not like about work. Major shifts in expectations have led to a more empowered workforce, with people demanding a work experience and reality closer to what they envisioned before joining the workforce: closer to their "dream job." Over the past few decades, we have been increasingly de-conditioned from being loyal employees and are more likely to act as free-agents, adjusting what we do for work according to our lives and priorities at a particular point in time. The growth of access to temporary and contract work, coupled with a relatively low unemployment rate, has provided the structural conditions to enable this more fluid work environment.

It is not just that short-term work can be accessed more easily that has been a trigger for more churn at work: people's personal priorities have vastly changed. A few generations ago, salary and the benefits of a good work pension were uppermost in many people's minds as they embarked on a career. Over time, work contracts have become materially less generous for many people when compared to the past, in particular in regard to pensions and job security. As a result of pensions being far less generous and jobs being far less secure, people no longer feel that they have a big enough incentive to stick around in a job they might not like.

It is not solely pragmatism about the package available though, for many people money is not the be all and end all anymore. As people have become much more concerned about well-being and quality of life, time, flexibility, and a culture that results in less personal stress are seen as vastly more important in individuals' decisions about where they work and how long they stay for. From "Generation X" forward, experiences are seen by many to be the new currency. As people have been successively priced out of the traditional "rites of passage" of ownership, they attribute far more importance to personal experiences, their own self-worth, and living for the moment than in previous times. This can create conflicts between the priorities of organizations and the people who work within them.

So, expectations about the way that we work have changed. This change includes not only the jobs that we do but also the time we spend at work, where we work, and the relationship we have with work itself. In a complete reversal from social attitudes of the past, people are increasingly no longer defining themselves by their jobs and are willing to forgo monetary rewards for more intangible quality of life factors such as time, location, flexibility, and a coherence with their own value systems. For some people, work is an opportunity to be with their "tribe," reinforcing their own sense of identity. Whereas in the past, your tribe was likely to be people within your work sector; now it is likely to be people who hold similar interests and views about leisure activities, ideologies, campaign interests, or well-being. Interest groups are now highly self-reinforcing via social media, and the connection to other people with our identity is likely to be far stronger than work bonds for many people.

This set of changes brings with it a sense of opportunity for some people and some organizations but also confusion and trepidation for others. Working in a more fluid way and meeting the work demands and expectations of new generations does not always sit so easily with old, established ways of managing people or organizing workflow. Organizations are not used to people making decisions about their employment at odds with what seems rationale in terms of conventional thinking. For example, why would someone reject an opportunity because of the way that they feel about relatively minor issues (in corporate terms) such as working on-site for three days rather than two, or because a company invests in areas that the potential employee feels is ethically not in line with their identity? Yet these scenarios are becoming increasingly common.

Many managers are familiar with aiming for best practice under traditional systems of operational leadership, keeping fairly static teams of people on-track with linear projects, working in one field with others of a similar background. They may be used to managing teams of people who accept the routine of coming in to a set workplace five days a week, where they have a direct and personal line of communication with all its subtleties and hierarchical norms and expectations. In short, they are used to being in charge of people they can see are "doing the job" with the manager/worker relationship traditionally defined. Remote working arrangements strongly challenge these assumptions and can challenge traditional managers.

Alongside expectation, the skills needed for work have changed in a revolutionary way. Smarter software and digital advantage will often drive competitive advantage for companies and organizations. Digital upskilling and digital dexterity are absolutely key components of arguably the majority of jobs. In the face of this need, it doesn't matter if someone has 1 year experience in an industry or 20 years, what matters more is their ability to handle technology. People unable to work with digital technology are already excluded from many sectors and certainly from senior jobs in almost any sector.

As work has become remote, it has increasingly become across countries, cultures, and even across languages in a way that was unthinkable in the Noughties. Technology (such as translation software) has made real-time communication across the globe easier than ever. People now work with the greatest diversity of colleagues imaginable, either physically or online. This may lead to challenges in terms of cross-cultural understanding for managers and colleagues alike.

The need for work to be meaningful and fit the value system of workers is now a "thing"; indeed, it is a very big thing. In many cases, employees want their organization to make a social impact. Coupled with the relative reduction in loyalty to one organization and the end of the expectation of employees to remain unconditionally loyal to one employer, this makes the culture of organizations across most industries absolutely critical to worker retention. The relationship that people have with those guiding them (managers and leaders) is under scrutiny like never before.

It is how people behave that matters. How people behave at work. How effectively they perform. How people accept or reject managerial behavior. How people feel about themselves in relation to others (including management) in this transition. Understanding how people behave is the key to managing different configurations of work successfully, and yet, this is the missing piece of the puzzle: at present, management is kind of doing the same thing but remotely. This needs to change.

To summarize, I cannot overstate the importance of norms and expectations in the way that work will be conducted and managed now and in the future. We now live in a world where we have very different expectations of what an organization offers. Think about what we expect as customers nowadays. We take it for granted that customer service will adhere to the "customer is always right" policy, that we will have 24-hour access to many services such as food delivery, and that we will be able to feedback on the services that we receive (including on our employers via services such as Glassdoor). We rate products and services and choose what we spend money and time on by looking at the way that other people have rated things, so awards, feedback sites, and public opinion in general are more important than ever. The customer is in control like never before in history. This coupled with a very strong employment market equates to quite a bit of power potentially in the hands of employees and a need for business and organizations to respond in terms of the way that people work and are managed.

Why We Want
Remote Work

The reasons why people prefer to work at home will vary. Research shows some common themes in terms of intangible and tangible benefits and costs. I'll run through some of the pretty obvious ones.

Improved work-life balance is at top of the list for most people, with strong crossovers into better well-being. Flexibility to at least partly restructure the working day according to your own situation has made an enormous difference to the lives of people who work remotely. There is a greatly increased awareness about the importance of work-life balance, especially as a way of strengthening family life and improving health. At a time when people feel more stressed than ever before, taking time away from work "recovery time" is seen as a strong antidote to work-induced burnout. Recovery time refers to time every day when you can remove yourself from work, even for a short period.

Work-life balance does not necessarily mean doing shorter hours. It means restructuring work to fit in with personal interests and family life. This could include deferring work outside the regular nine-to-five day for work which can theoretically be done at any time. Structuring work to your own priorities and thereby gaining improved work-life balance may have strong benefits in terms of well-being when it comes to gaining a sense of control over your life. The common problem of work issues impacting on life issues is reduced.

As well as gaining more balance in their lives, people want to cut out sources of stress. A major source of stress that many of us will recognize is the urban commute. This scourge of on-site work is hated world over and is not exclusive to people who drive, although it can feel particularly soul-destroying battling through traffic queues to arrive, emotionally shattered, at work. People value the extra time saved and the stress reduced by not needing to travel. The average daily commute time in the

UK is 59 minutes[1]—in many cases that is just "stress-generating time." If you compare being stuck on an A road for an hour with spending that time going for a stroll round a local park and then settling into your home-office, you will appreciate the potential benefits of remote work.

Although it is possible to work on a train or even on a bus safely, for most people, commuting is "dead" time and certainly time which offers no productivity advantage to simply working from a space in your own home. (I am not including the potential of walking as a form of commuting, which may offer productivity advantages and well-being advantages but is undertaken by a very small proportion of commuters.) Cutting out the commute frees people to use saved commuting time as they want and also frees them from the necessity of living within commutable distance. This may be true even for hybrid working as people may decide that they are willing to take one long commute per week, for example, in order to live where they want to. Being free of having to commute can be incredibly empowering for people.

Dispensing with commuting is not just a win for workers either. Saved commuting time may mean higher quality work, achievable because people are not feeling worn out and stressed by their journeys: a big win for organizations.

There are concrete savings to be made too. At a time of steeply rising costs, this is a major attraction of remote working for many people. Savings soon mount up if you don't have to go to your organization's premises to work. If you previously had to commute a long way and also spend quite a bit on refreshments while at work, you will save money both on travel and discretionary retail spend (popping out for a coffee/muffin/sushi, etc.). Of course, this cuts both ways: you might end up still popping out and spending more than you used to (and more than you can claim back in tax allowances) on things such as heating, better broadband, extra treats, or even a pet to keep you company. The money you save or spend as a result of remote working will depend on individual circumstances.

---

[1] www.tuc.org.uk/news/annual-commuting-time-21-hours-compared-decade-ago-finds-tuc.

There are other location-based benefits that might apply to relatively small numbers of people at the moment, but which may change the "norm" for how work is undertaken for larger numbers over time. If you can work from anywhere with an Internet connection, there is nothing stopping you from working from your second home abroad, or on holiday, or even on the road. Certainly, you can work for a company in an entirely different country from your own home. With many people loving to globetrot, the attraction of combining work with travel is clear, although perhaps only a reality for the lucky few at present.

For some people, working remotely is more of an ethical issue linked to climate change. At a societal level, less commuting equals less pollution. Cast your mind back to the 2020 lockdown and much was made of the massive reduction in pollution in China and elsewhere. Post lockdown, the contrast with a pre-Covid world will be less dramatic; however, there may still be gains in terms of less pollution and less fossil fuel use if people choose not to use cars as much as they used to now they are working in a hybrid or remote way, or if they become more energy conscious in general.

Advocates of remote work, contrary to early beliefs painting them as looking for a way to get away with working less hard, actually mainly *want* to be productive and see remote working as the best way to achieve this. About two-thirds of workers subjectively feel that they would be more productive in a home office than a business office. Remote work can enable better productivity and performance through reducing distractions: compared to the 101 things going on around you in an office, you can really concentrate on the task in hand when working remotely. This argument has its limitations though—when life and its everyday (or even manufactured) distractions interfere with work, the balance can tip the other way. Who hasn't started off with good intentions when sitting at a computer and ended up "researching" the news or something interesting on Ebay?

Fewer distractions also create an atmosphere more conducive to creative, divergent thinking. People can access a wider range of potential inspiration, or feel free to conduct research at a time that suits them rather than an employer, for example.

For some groups of people, such as those with caring responsibilities, working from home means access to work that would previously have been unavailable because of restrictions on their time and mobility. This means that hybrid- and home-working extends access to employment and better employment to underrepresented groups such as parents with child care responsibilities. This is an important contribution to equality and diversity.

Very important in my opinion are the wants and needs that people have from remote work that are identical to what they expect from on-site work: self-respect, mental stimulation, companionship, personal growth—aspects that are dependent upon relationships, management, and culture. It is these factors that may be the most challenging to provide in a remote working environment, yet for most people, these are still key priorities for work. The physical separation of us from others is what makes these emotional and psychological needs more challenging to deliver. In fact, remote work, as currently managed, does not deliver on these needs effectively. That is not to say that people working remotely always end up worse off—as ever it depends on individual circumstances.

In some cases, work relations may improve. Some workers feel that they get on better with others if they are working remotely. This could be because people may be less interested in the lives of people met less frequently and therefore are less likely to engage in office politics. It could be because some people actively foster online contact with people they get on with and try and filter out people that might cause them stress. It could just be that they feel more refreshed and calmer generally and therefore are more inclined to get on with people. It could even be a generational thing, with younger people conditioned to feel far more comfortable interacting via screens than in-person.

So, there are a number of very compelling practical reasons that justify home and hybrid working from workers' perspectives. They are the headline reasons; but the important and unappreciated reasons why people prefer to work from home also include issues that speak more of poor management in general than the merits of one location over another. Working remotely means being able to keep physically away from people you don't like. If micromanagement was an issue in your life, remote working can give you space away from managers breathing down your neck.

Many people now feel less secure about being in group environments, for reasons ranging from Covid anxiety to being naturally shy or conditioned out of mixing with people through spending much of their time online with friends. Remote working naturally allows people to remain separate from others. It can also mean that people can "hide" away for the majority of the time, just popping up for the odd team meeting now and then. This might not be a widespread problem; however, some people will take an active opportunity to avoid scrutiny (just as happens with on-site work). Identifying and minimizing misuse of remote working arrangements will be a consideration for managers.

To summarize, people want a wide range of benefits from remote working. Better work-life balance, convenience, savings in costs, greater autonomy, more time, and reduced stress are some of the primary goals. Increasingly, people also just feel that remote working makes sense: if work can be conducted from home, then why should there be any problem with that?

It is not just on the employee side that the benefits of remote working have been acknowledged. More than three-quarters of UK businesses operating remote working surveyed by the ONS in 2022 gave improved staff well-being as a reason for using home working permanently, the spin off being less time off because of ill health. Employers also noted reduced overheads, for example, if they stopped renting premises if employees were contracted to work at home. Productivity also increased.

A growing factor for employers, given that more and more people are not able (perhaps because they have moved to a remote location) or willing to undertake office-based work, is the realization that they will attract higher caliber workers, from a wider and deeper talent pool (both UK and internationally) if they offer remote working. (This is more limited with hybrid working setups.) This talent issue has been recognized by a growing number of leaders of professional firms, and in my view, firms in the race for global talent will have no option but to offer remote working to match the offer of their global competitors.

Remote Working Downsides

The work landscape has been remodeled with a strong orientation toward hybrid and remote work, but the switch is not without its detractors. The pros of remote working are easy to see but there are a few realities about remote working that should be considered in order to optimize the benefits for both employer and recruiter. The very rapid shift to working remotely has not, in my view, taken account of the basics of behavior. Remote and especially hybrid working can be very successful ways of organizing work; however, just doing what used to be done but moving that to being remote is not the best model, either for managers or workers.

Managing remote working means understanding a number of risks: behavioral, psychological, and organizational. This can be successfully done, but with such a dramatic shift to this style of working, this needs a lot more work to get it right.

So, what are the pitfalls with remote working? Increased use of the technology and reduced in-person contact underpin many of the behavioral changes that create potential problems. We behave very differently working from home to the way we would if we were sitting in an office with other people. A virtual office is not a real office.

It is widely acknowledged that a very significant problem could be loneliness and isolation. The very environment that is considered important to successful home working—a dedicated space without interruption from other people—could, ironically, create a sense of isolation and potentially have a negative impact on mental health. Some people deal well with being totally cut off, but most of us need to interact with others to maintain good psychological health. Interacting online cannot fully replace the genuine interaction we have when in the physical presence of colleagues. Work is where many people have the bulk of their social interactions, and with far fewer opportunities to meet people in the real world even in the years prior to Covid because of life moving increasingly online, we were already starting to feel lonelier.

The increasing prevalence of poor mental health and resilience among younger people prior to Covid was already being blamed on the growing isolation people have from each other. Increasing dependency on social media is the driver for an unrealistic image of how life is supposed to be, and this can leave people feeling inadequate and lonely. It can also lead to expectations of instant gratification and a reduced ability to deal with emotions.

If people do not have an opportunity to form real work relationships and friendships from an early stage in their career, it is far from certain that the gaps will be filled by outside work relationships and people may suffer in terms of poor mental health without even recognizing that it is because of social and work isolation.

At a time when social resiliency is ebbing, increasing remote work might further fracture bonds in a work community. For some people, having no sense of work community may be a serious detriment to mental health, perhaps only noticeable when an individual is confronted by a challenge in a work or nonwork situation. Isolation can have an insidious effect that is often not noticeable until something reminds people of how things used to be and they can compare their pre- and postisolation feelings and behavior. The inability to cope can be linked to loneliness and isolation.

This is not to say that everyone that works remotely will feel lonely or isolated, but this can become a problem even for people who initially see remote working as an ideal work scenario for themselves. Some people find that after a period of time without actively going into work and mixing with other people, they can start to behave in uncharacteristically insecure ways.

Often, you don't know that something is wrong until you can contrast it with something better. During lockdown, when working at home became compulsory for many people, the negative side effects of working remotely gnawed away at some people without them realizing. Distress can build up over time without our conscious awareness and it is when we feel happy, or creative or positive again when we are back with other people that we can see that being cut off from work colleagues and environments may have a dark side. During lockdowns, the initial gratitude to be able to work, or to help society, was not enough to counter the natural need that we had for human companionship and connection: pretty soon many people started to get cabin fever. For people with a good social network, the impact may have been less, but for the many people living alone, or with people with whom they did not get on too well, remote working became the source of isolation and stress. Where people lived influenced the response to remote working too: if you lived in a peaceful and green area, remote working (interspersed with walks in the countryside) was probably less of a burden than for people living in a congested apartment in a dense city without access to a garden. However, whatever the character of your surroundings, working where you live, with few opportunities to physically mix with other people, could become an express route to loneliness, the hidden epidemic behind the pandemic.

It is a fact that remote work causes loneliness. In research about remote work among journalists conducted more than a decade before the pandemic, the organizational psychologist Lynn Holdsworth found that full-time telework increased loneliness over office work by 67 percent.[1] In new sectors (such as working with social media) where remote work was already fairly popular before the pandemic, loneliness was already identified as a major side effect of working remotely. Loneliness can have business impacts, including employee burnout and turnover, so the implications of getting things wrong with managing remote work can be serious from both a personal and organizational perspective.

It matters whether you self-select into remote work or not. People who thrive on flexibility and have an existing active social and professional network are more likely to relish remote working than those who have not previously had the opportunity to form face-to-face relationships with colleagues. One of the main gaps is the absence of much of the regular opportunities to create a sense of belonging. When we move around a workplace, we do more than get from A to B. The paths that we take when going to get a coffee from the kitchen or on the way to a meeting create functional inconvenience that give us a chance to catch up informally with others. It is these encounters that, over time, make us all

---

[1] https://www.researchgate.net/publication/229525709_The_Psychological_Impact_of_Teleworking_Stress_Emotions_and_Health.

feel a bond with our colleagues. Even if we don't really like some people, this familiarity is comforting at a deep, psychological level. Think of all the times you've shared a knowing look with a workmate when someone has behaved in a predictably embarrassing way, and you will understand that these acquired understandings develop over time and mean a lot. If people don't feel a sense of belonging where they work, they are more likely to consider leaving and going elsewhere. In a world where loyalty to an employer is diminishing generally, this is another blow to the challenge of retaining the best workers.

Poorly managed, working remotely can be the slippery slope to people "disappearing." Being out of sight, it is very easy to be "out of mind" which carries many potential risks, from shirking work and working to a poor standard because of a lack of guidance or interest on the part of management, to serious mental health issues.

It is not impossible to build work relationships in an online-only environment; it is just a lot more difficult. Relationships are hard enough to build and maintain in traditional working environments. When relationships are moved, online relationship-building becomes very much harder. If colleagues are dotted all over the world and therefore not likely to ever meet face-to-face, it is easy to see that there may emerge a hierarchy of affiliation to colleague relationships based on factors such as physical proximity that might not be great for work outcomes. The more remote we are from other people in terms of identity the more we tend to discount their views rather than respect them. This lack of empathy can be damaging both for workers and organizations.

Misunderstandings can arise when we don't have the nonverbal cues in a conversation and remove the potential for new ideas to be sparked by face-to-face conversations. It is as well to remind ourselves of some of the reasons why people have resisted remote working in the past—the social benefits of interacting with people in the office and the risk of working long hours at home without the moderating influence of a set time to physically leave a workplace.

When you are not physically with your work colleagues, it can be difficult working out whether you can trust them. Online, most of us try and put on a professional persona and we are usually some distance from being ourselves. Of course, face-to-face, people can also hold back, but it is a lot easier to determine if someone is being genuine, if they are on our wavelength and on our side about matters than when interaction is online. Online encounters feel, by necessity, suspicious and bland. Because we tend to be more cautious online, we spend a lot of time second-guessing whether we can trust others (reinforced by general messages we internalize about the dangers of online information), so it is very hard to work out who your real allies are. Work is where we regularly need allies to back us in all sorts of scenarios, from the trivial to the important. Without the feeling of security knowing that we can rely on specific people for support brings, we are far less likely to say what we mean or take reasonable work risks. Coupled with the misunderstandings that may arise out of online messaging, you can easily see the problem of not knowing where you stand with your remote work colleagues.

Working remotely has unlocked the potential of video chat and meetings, predominantly over platforms like Zoom, Teams, or Skype. This has heralded the existence of so-called Zoom fatigue where we feel drained after a succession of video meetings. The reason for feeling so done-in is that we actually use a lot of processing power to watch and understand everything that is going on in video calls, and our brains can't help but try and take in the huge amount of visual information present. Unconsciously "looking too hard" not only drains your brain, it can also cloud your judgment as you react to how people look rather than what they are saying. This is also a well-recognized risk in face-to-face encounters of course, and we should be using opportunities to reduce appearance bias in any way we can.

A range of other communications problems can present themselves when we switch to mainly online messaging as our main method of work communication. Team chats/Slack, and so on can become repositories of online low-level cyber-bullying when people are left out of conversations or become subject to spite, sometimes even through the use of emojis. The potential for misunderstandings in online chat can be very high, and there is a possibility that this leads to poor personal and working outcomes.

Although productivity is generally not an issue when working remotely, some people might struggle. The fundamental way we work is increasingly dependent on being multiplatform, multinetwork, and multimedia.

Without proper training and management, we can fool ourselves into thinking that the more browsers we have open at once the more productive, important, and dynamic we are. This becomes an issue when working remotely as we can fall into a trap of appearing to be productive rather than actually being productive using "evidence" of having lots of tabs open and looking like we are doing "stuff." Coincidentally, it has been proved that genuine multitasking is not possible: your brain can only focus or concentrate effectively on one thing at a time—filtering out all the other "noise." Asking your brain to do more than this means that performance drops across all the tasks we try to do simultaneously.

Concentration is another attribute that has the potential to be profoundly affected by the switch to tech-led remote work. Technology has enabled us to access more information than ever before and zip between different information, often presented in potted snippet form, for ease of use. This conditions us to switch off and stop concentrating much sooner than with in-person events. Already our concentration has been waning as we instinctively seek out shorter and shorter ways to receive information. We tend to switch off after about 10 minutes, meaning that we struggle to maintain attention on video calls.

This brings us to the subject of validation. We need validation at work of course. Without the positive reinforcement that people get from being around other people at work, there is a risk of people clinging to the sort of validation that might result from Teams' chat emojis rather than something more meaningful. Validation at work needs to be carefully considered so that it does not revert to a social-media scenario of anticipating and counting "likes."

Remote work must deal with the inevitable problems that come with technology breakdown. From not being able to operate a microphone on a Zoom call to a complete hardware failure, there will regularly be IT problems. This creates stress. There are few things as stressful as being on an important call and you lose connection, even the most seasoned professional will feel some embarrassment and the repercussions could be serious work-wise. Learning how to be resilient when faced with these kinds of issues is an important feature for remote workers. When technology malfunctions, we exhibit all the frustrations that our brains have evolved to display as part of the drive to discover solutions. The problem is that often we *can't find* solutions to technology problems ourselves, or even know how to fill the time usefully when a problem occurs—often leaving us floundering around waiting for help rather than doing something constructive.

Finally, there are some practical outcomes that working remotely can have. Work has traditionally been imbued with subtle rituals that reinforce our sense of self-esteem and clarify that we have a purpose and routine to our day. Although parodied, not having to make an effort to get dressed to go to work can leave people feeling slovenly and affect mood. Dressing smartly has a positive effect on morale and helps people to value themselves and look forward to meeting others. Making an effort is something that we enjoy doing.

Working at home all day means that we may not have the need to do the exercise we used to as part of our regular working day: the walking to transport or around the office. It also means that we have access to any goodies hiding in our kitchen cupboards or fridge. Both of these situations can result in us losing fitness and potentially putting on weight—as many people did during the first UK lockdown when working at home was compulsory for many.

For some people, there are fewer distractions at home, but for others, there are more. Working remotely needs self-discipline and self-motivation to focus, to avoid distractions and to be productive. Distraction can range from the banal to the harmful. Being out of sight can trigger other habits that are potentially harmful. Lockdown ushered in a new breed of armchair "investor" putting their money into risky assets via commission-free apps. This type of investment is part of a wider shift to financial investment egalitarianism in that anyone can do it without financial advice or knowledge. Unfortunately, investing in this way, like gambling, is risky and can be addictive. Having the technology, the time, and the privacy to take risks with money has resulted in serious financial loss for some remote workers.

Other people have stumbled into home-office-based drinking or smoking, watching porn, or other illicit activities that presumably they would not have undertaken in their regular workplace. Though rare, these behaviors can be reality when remote work is not thought through and managed well.

Our brains work in primitive ways; we can't help subconsciously reacting to our environment in ways that are outside our control. Remote working runs counter to our human trait to need company and can lead to pernicious loneliness and depression. Left to our own devices, we can also fall into bad habits—from being slovenly to becoming addicted to various vices. Perhaps, the office really does have something going for it after all?

The next section of the book will consider how organizations and the dynamics within them may have changed forever as a result of remote and hybrid work. It will also explore how there is a worrying lack of thought into managing remote work effectively, despite this being the biggest upheaval to working lives in living memory for most people.

Managing in the Remote Work Era

New Power Dynamics

Remote work arrangements have caused arguably the biggest shake-up to power relationships at work in memory, and it has happened so quickly.

During the COVID-19 period, frontline workers worked from their place of work whereas managers worked from home. This meant a virtual disconnect between colleagues, either across the entire organization, or between levels within an organization. The impact of this disconnect on relationships should not be underestimated and may have long-term implications of widening perceived status inequalities. It remains to be seen how power relationships will change after many remote workers proved themselves able to work effectively with a much reduced level of management.

Organizations will need to adapt to new realities. They may be compelled to cede power to people who have proved themselves in the remote-working environment. This can free up leaders to identify how to create organizational cultures with new ways of participating across the board, bringing together both remote and place-based working—a major challenge for the future. Post-Covid, leaders will need to lead a newly empowered, perhaps anxious workforce during a turbulent phase of history when jobs and sectors radically change and the specter of new virus outbreaks persists.

The big game changer in the remote/hybrid/office debate is self-determination. The striving for increased self-control is central to the way that many of us plan our lives and careers. By moving up the career ladder, we are ultimately trying to gain more control over our lives, whether this is by having more power at work or simply more money to open up our options in life. The changes brought about by the unique circumstances of the Covid Pandemic fundamentally disrupted relationships between different areas of work and different working setups. The emergence into a new reality of work sectors and design is a continuing process of resetting norms, hierarchies, and power relationships.

The mass shift to remote work has turned power relationships at work upside down. The lack of comprehension of the scale of the change and how to respond positively is the single most striking weakness in management today and the greatest challenge organizations face.

During lockdowns, when remote working was mandated, there was no choice in where to work: if you could work from home, this is where you worked, the alternative being to be furloughed (in the UK). This compulsion, a feeling that we had no choice in the matter, coupled with fierce restrictions in movement and mixing with other people, led to considerable anxiety about working from home in the very early days. Workers thought they might not be able to do their jobs very well and that they would be caught out in some way, and managers felt that they would be faced with teams of people unable to do the job properly or who would shirk rather than work at home. People also, naturally, felt a great deal of anxiety about the risk of Covid and suffered the stresses that come with being involuntarily cut off from family, friends, and work colleagues. Hybrid work was not a thing during lockdown: you either worked from home or went in to work, so the contrast between industries and types of work was stark.

At the start of lockdown, many people saw remote work as likely to be a very short-term disaster for organizations and the economy. Reality proved to be very different. The adjustment to remote working was swift and remarkable. It became clear that organizations were able to keep functioning and work *was* able to be transferred, with the help of technology, to the home environment with little loss of production. In some cases, an entire organization went remote, or just the elements that were able to be undertaken remotely—essentially managerial and administrative functions that could be undertaken via online methods. It was clear that remote working was not a disaster. The genie was out of the bottle.

When work is stripped down to its basics it is about completing tasks, it does not matter where those tasks are completed. If you have a report to write, arguably it doesn't matter if it is completed in an office or in the bath. If you have meetings to hold, it doesn't matter if these are in a corporate office or on Zoom. Curiously, across the board, work was completed, on time, and to a high standard when people worked from home during Covid. People did not end up lost and confused; they got on with their jobs to a high standard and often more efficiently than they had back at the office. People did this while being managed remotely.

The transfer of management to being remote has been interesting. Managers were not used to managing remotely. It was therefore a steep learning curve for many to learn the technology and then mainly guess at what would be the best way to manage teams and conduct business. At a time when the country was in crisis, learning the best way to manage online was not a top priority for most managers, who went into "self-interpretation of the situation" mode. The results were variable.

For a great many workers who knew their jobs well, it became clear that being managed was not the essential component of productivity that it had been assumed to be. Many people could just get on with the job unsupervised. On the other side of the fence, there were plenty of examples of dreadful management.

Poorly managed team meetings online were sometimes stark examples of awkward silence or unprofessional shows of immaturity from senior people, as made popular by the now infamous Handforth Parish Council meeting video. There was something about online one-to-ones that made people want to press "leave" as soon as possible and go back to doing the job. Online team chat enabled people to expose and joke about managerial misgivings with their work colleagues and even question the value of having a manager at all.

There was a fast-emerging realization that working remotely can bring greater autonomy for less senior personnel. Virtual meetings exposed the limitations of being stuck online, as people experienced the awkward futility of trying to replicate in-person networking. People quickly found workarounds to aspects of remote meetings that they disliked; the ability to turn cameras off and be on mute gives people a degree of control that is not possible when in the office and was a great option in the eyes of many. These small details added to the transfer of power away from people who had succeeded by being well-networked or good at office politics (or at repackaging other people's work as their own, or even just good at avoiding blame) and toward the people lower down in traditional hierarchies who actually produce measureable work.

As noted, productivity improved when work went remote, and more surprisingly, it has stayed higher than when the same work was undertaken in-office. It was no surprise to psychologists that productivity initially rose because remote work was a novelty for most people and novelty tends to lead to performance gains. For productivity to stay elevated though points to other, deeper factors such as the self-organization of people into smaller, more logical working teams (which tend to be more productive), and their move into self-managing work—the real bombshell of the remote work revolution.

Working remotely has made people see first-hand that the value of managers, especially to the bottom line, may be overblown. Away from the office environment where managers can "prove" their importance by looking important or being continuously busy with meetings, the ego-driven management style breaks down. Without much input at all from managers, workers have calmly negotiated organizing and delivering on their own work, often maturely dealing with managerial deficiencies along the way.

With fewer hiding places for management failings, remote work has also revealed the problems that managers have often swept under the carpet because they either don't have the ability to deal with them or because they don't have the inclination—issues like ensuring that people have stimulating work or are treated with respect.

It has also revealed the ability of people who in their former in-person environment may have been underestimated and overlooked because they are not people who engage in the politics of being liked by the right people as a way to progress. It has conversely disadvantaged people who are not very good at their jobs but have relied upon sucking up to the right people. Remote work has the ability to rebalance the scales in favor of people who "do" rather than act the part.

Office environments are perfect for ego-driven management, with all its insecurity and personal microaggressions. Too often, managers have relied on their ability to exert their power informally by choosing whom to communicate with and communicating behind closed doors in the knowledge that they will not be held to account. When communication can be recorded via Zoom or Teams, or is downloadable from Slack or another chat app, people have to reassess what they say.

Less obviously, within a physical office, there is unconscious bias that can mean that different groups of people are stereotyped because of their identity and hierarchies of importance attributed by characteristics like gender, race, or age rather than actual ability or results. Simply by turning a camera off, a whole swathe of potential stereotyping disappears. Remotely, a female engineer or an older social media marketer can silence assumptions simply by doing great work, while others who were assumed to be the best may be revealed as better at blagging than getting results.

A remote environment provides an opportunity to question just what management is and assess whether it actually adds value. If the role of management has been to collect work and pass it on, is this really adding value: why can't someone send their work on themselves and miss out the middle-man? It might be hard to see potentially more efficient ways of doing things when we work in offices where we don't have a clear line of sight into what others are doing. It becomes a lot easier to see inefficiencies when we can see who produces or does not produce work: this reveals effective ways to get to an endpoint and practices that do not add value, perhaps even making things less efficient or increasing the potential for errors. Of course, the potential for obfuscation exists online also; however, it is a lot easier to see where the gaps are.

If management is about linking people together and coordinating action, the effectiveness of many managers to do this remotely has been suspect, with people, once aware of the needs of their role, able to work more effectively by communicating directly and in a more relaxed and partnership-oriented way with others in the organization. Given the tools to do this (a messaging app), people have proved that they can take the initiative and manage their own work by engaging directly with peers. Workflow platforms with clear dashboards give people the ability to gauge their own performance against leader-boards and targets and even suggest steps that they can take to concentrate on areas of weakness. As people become increasingly adept at taking charge of their own work, the presence of managers who appear to have less of an impact on the work and certainly contribute less in terms of measurable output becomes less justifiable. The role of a manager needs to be urgently reimagined given the new reality that remote work brings.

Remote working removes much of the infrastructure that has built up managerial territories of control and disrupts the way that management is viewed by workers in their teams in some cases. It has led to a shift in power relations, linked to a new willingness to question how people and environments do or do not add value to work.

As the transition out of the Covid-dominated era continues, more reflection needs to be devoted to the impact of a changed work reality on power relationships at work and not just in relation to scenarios where both managers and workers are working remotely. There are many sectors where people have to be physically present, for example, hospitality or transport, manufacturing, or care. In some cases, frontline workers have been working on-site, whereas managers have been working from home and will continue working from home in many cases. This has meant that there has been a disconnect between colleagues, either across the entire organization or between levels within an organization. The impact of this disconnect on relationships should not be underestimated. Feelings of unfairness at work are very impactful on morale and performance, and the existence of different rules for different levels of a hierarchy is likely to cause problems.

Accusations of hypocrisy can be directed at organizational leaders extolling the need for people to return to the office environment, while simultaneously continuing to work remotely themselves for the vast majority of time. If anything, logic dictates that managers and leaders should be the ones present in corporate premises even if the majority of staff members are working remotely, since this enables them to show their own commitment to making personal sacrifices to lead in a visible way.

Creating a High-Trust Environment

When workers are left to manage themselves, as happened as a result of managerial vacuums when managers stepped back from effectively managing remote teams, either because of lack of awareness or ability or because team members proved better at directing their own work, unexpected consequences can emerge which further erode traditional top-down power relationships. Remote work can lead to a type of self-selection of matrix like teams by people within the teams themselves—with no managerial input. This happens when people use their knowledge and initiative to work out who needs to be involved in a particular piece of work or project; it is no surprise that someone doing a job knows exactly what is needed to do it effectively and without the problems that can creep in as a result of well-intentioned managerial input that looks good on paper but lacks knowledge of what happens in reality. From administration to complex projects, it is the people doing the work who have proven that they know the most effective team to construct and the clearest path to a goal. This is an example of people "free-styling" their own way of work. Although free-styling does have limitations, for example, when people need to move to tasks beyond their current experience, it is easy to see how harnessing this natural initiative can lead to a rapid escalation in self-belief.

It is no surprise that some people have questioned the need for management at all if productivity, efficiencies, and peer relationships are better when managers are off the scene. However, upholding and managing participation and delivery is a big remote working managerial remit since remote work carries many behavioral and well-being risks as I have mentioned. The need for good management is very much alive.

Rather than resort to trying to impose the old ways which have been proved irrelevant given the social experiment that Covid has enabled, an alternative is for managers to use the opportunity to adapt to new realities.

This can free up leaders to identify how to create a new organizational culture with new ways of participating across the board—a major challenge for the future. In the coming era of remote and hybrid working, leaders will need to lead a newly empowered workforce during a turbulent phase of history when jobs and sectors radically change and the specter of new virus outbreaks persists. This is a time for humility and acceptance. You may not have been as important as you thought you were, but there is now an opportunity to lead like never before.

Many company executives have voiced concern that too much remote work time will destroy corporate culture that has taken decades to develop and they don't want to lose. The fact is that employees seem less bothered about aspects of the corporate culture, or may see a direct lack of congruence between stated corporate values and not offering more flexibility and autonomy to staff. They feel that remote working has totally exposed the stupidity of physical "presenteeism" as part of workplace culture. Presenteeism is the killer of productivity, the unwritten rule that you turn up to a desk, and look as if you are working, even if you are doing no work. As long as you are at your desk, you will have ticked a box marking you as being in line with expectations. If you remain at your desk for long hours without doing much (perhaps because you are burnt out), you will probably still be credited with being a devoted and hard-working team member. Showing up for the sake of it can fulfill a psychological need for the employee, while managers, unaware of what workers are actually doing, they assume that value is being added. Presenteeism is caused by feeling compelled to "show up" at work and is a real productivity killer.

Surveillance is closely associated with presenteeism. This can be via the measurement of work being done, which is legitimate of course, especially early on in careers. It can also be via excessive monitoring by our peers and managers. It is when surveillance makes us feel obliged, uncomfortable, and micromanaged that it leads to problems.

People also subconsciously or actively adopt presenteeism because they have more visibility in the eyes of their peers and seniors and therefore grow in affinity with them, leading to their being more likely to be viewed favorably just for being present. Presenteeism in fact can promote unconscious bias.

Presenteeism is transferrable to remote work, of course. Being logged-on is not the same as engaging in productive work. The temptation to engage in presenteeism is just as strong if you are working remotely and arguably more so, since you can be logged-on but watching a film instead of doing any work. You can also be working remotely for far more than your scheduled hours and suffer burnout just as easily as in the office, if not more so.

The opposite of the sort of culture within which presenteeism thrives is one where people are left to their own devices, with the expectation that they will deliver the goods anyway. Presenteeism is there because of a lack of trust: people are not felt to be trustworthy enough to get on with things as they see fit, without being watched. Remote working provides the environment to test the premise that people can't be trusted and replace this with an inherent belief that people, properly managed and valued, will perform their work in a mature and trustworthy way, with the need for surveillance.

Silo-working, where people tend to keep things within their own workgroup, with different workgroups not really communicating, is another side effect of a low-trust environment. Silo-working is a well-known source of duplication, wasted effort, and frustration, but despite being acknowledged to be a major cause of poor outcomes in organizations, it continues. Silos are maintained by defensive and distrusting managers and poor communicators so it figures that improving communication and removing poor management will increase collaboration and reduce silos; remote working creates this opportunity.

Creating a high-trust environment, where people are left to organize work within their own flexible boundaries, challenges the traditional power relationships that have been accepted in one form or another since humanity began. Just drawing up contracts allowing people to work flexibly, be that fully remote or hybrid, is not enough. This is a time to take stock of changed realities and "facts on the ground," appreciate that power relationships have changed in the world of work and then start considering how corporate culture needs to change to move with rather than against progress, using the opportunity to consider how organizations deal with broader issues of performance, productivity, relationships, and essentially trust. We should be careful also not to throw the baby out with the bathwater: on-site working is not universally bad just as remote working is not a perfect way of working. Both systems have good and bad elements, and it is important to consider these so that we don't just end up with solutions that make work a worse experience for people.

As workers have started to comprehend that they actually do just as well working remotely and to some extent can manage themselves better when working in a more freestyle way, some people have gone further than express disappointment with on-site return: they have effectively refused to go back to a routine where they are committed full time to work on business premises rather than at least partly remotely. With an economy that has a low level of unemployment, it is workers who hold the cards at the moment and, newly empowered by evidence of their success when working remotely, may very well be able to deny employers who are seeking a return to fully on-site work for workers what they want. After all, if workers are not prepared to work for your organization unless it offers at least hybrid working arrangements, that is a very powerful motivation to offer it.

A reappraisal of organizational culture will enable us to think very practically about how the new working landscape will be managed, something that appears at present to be a very ad-hoc affair. Management will need to change. All of this will be challenging and, judging by the uncertainty around so many factors, will need to build in buffers of flexibility. It's the biggest opportunity to improve the productivity, fairness, and well-being orientation of organizations we have ever had.

The New Reality
for Organizations

Jobs and working environments have been changing since before Covid. The rapid acceptance of hybrid working arrangements and, to a lesser extent, totally remote work has exposed the lack of strategy on the part of organizations in deciding on which model to adopt. It has also revealed the absence of ability to handle this new way of working effectively by some managers and leaders and has even raised questions about the need for them in some cases.

Post-Covid feels like a different world for organizations, a tougher and more uncertain one. Organizations now operate in a world where work itself has a very different meaning and place in people's lives. Workers, sometimes with a cushion of savings, have taken individual decisions to move to different sectors, part-time rather than full-time, or leave the employed market altogether. Having reassessed their priorities during Covid, they now demand much more in terms of flexibility and synergy between their values and organizational culture.

The churn-in workers at present feels very different to times gone by. The very identity of a worker incorporates the potential to move smartly and responsively through work, focusing on individual priorities. A "work-hustle" mentality using social media to guide thinking has replaced the loyalty to employers that existed in earlier times. Some people are leaving just because they can and can see better opportunities on a rolling basis. Other people have decided that they are no longer prepared to put up with poor management or poor conditions. Some people have simply decided that they will be happier spending more time doing things that they have decided to prioritize over work.

As we have become more familiar with remote and hybrid work, we have begun to appreciate that working is not just about doing a job but about all of the culture, expectations, and aesthetics that go with it. Organizations have invested a lot into shared physical conditions that will keep people working, things like free food and an office gym. A lot of investment has been put into creating conditions designed to build loyalty and commitment, and it is easy to see how some employers may now be perturbed that many people are less impressed by the physical trappings of organizations and more concerned about policies that give them more control over their life, the most important of which being the right to have the choice to work remotely.

All of this equates to a set of changed realities for organizations, which they are quickly beginning to comprehend. Ideally, businesses and other organizations will take the time and trouble to build up their own strategic resilience so that they are prepared for future traumatic events after the example of the global Covid Pandemic. Realistically though, most organizations don't have the resources (especially with the specter of another global recession on the horizon) for crisis response teams and the like. Most are concerned with the here and now.

The here and now (and anticipating the future) is, to be frank, enough to be getting on with. Organizations are in a war to attract and keep good workers. The Great Resignation (United States)[1] did lead to an exodus of employees, but many of them have returned on their own terms rather than employer-led ones. In the current tight labor market, there is little to suggest that there will be any change to this, particularly since it makes sense for organizations to accept and benefit from the changes that workers now insist upon.

Organizations as well as managers need to, dare I say it, be more humble. By not assuming that they can dictate the rules of engagement, they will model the most strategically resilient organization possible—one that responds to the uncertainty that exists today. Even in a different environment, with fewer vacancies, the best people will always go to and stay at quality organizations. The good news for many smaller organizations is that the companies that will appeal to workers in the future are not necessarily those that pay the most, but those that make the lifestyle aspirations of their employees both at work and outside work possible. The days of working for the "biggest" are being replaced by the days of working for the "best for me."

---

[1] www.theguardian.com/business/2022/jan/04/great-resignation-quitting-us-unemployment-economy.

Offering remote and hybrid working should be an opportunity to think afresh about the overarching culture of an organization. The discussion should take an organization away from silo-working, low-trust micromanagement, and constraints on what employees can contribute to. Instead, it should embrace a strategy to encourage a cross-functional working and high-trust environment where people potentially have the freedom to demonstrate a greater range of skills.

Remote working is perhaps the starkest change that employers can offer in the new partnership-oriented era of work but it is not the only one. Changed realities on the ground dictate that organizations should dispense with master and servant mentality and adopt more partnership-oriented approaches, reflecting the changed power relationships that now exist.

Changed Realities on the Ground

What people want and expect now, compared to what they wanted and expected in the past, are too completely different that organizations need to think from the ground up about what they are offering people in order to attract and retain their goodwill and labor. Just as important as changed expectations are people's attitudes to life in general since these direct the way that they make decisions and behave in work and out of it. Of course, there is no such thing as a standard worker; people are individuals and different groups of people behave in different ways. I'll break workers down into more specific groups for the purpose of considering how to manage remote and hybrid working a little later. At present though, here are some generalizations.

People simply don't want to do some jobs. Call it entitlement or arrogance or just a recognition that working in some roles will be detrimental because of pay, conditions, or well-being. The end result is that large numbers of people will now automatically pass over jobs that they may have considered viable in the past. In some cases, people would rather be unemployed than do these jobs.

People's relationship with money has changed, but we still want money and feel entitled to it. People at the lower end of the income scale understandably place a lot of importance on monetary reward for work, since covering basic living costs is an issue. However, even low-paid workers place flexibility above the discomfort and inconvenience of working in the wrong place. The recruitment crisis in many industries in the UK post-Covid shows the strength of feeling that is behind people not returning to many traditional low-skilled jobs. It seems that some people now disregard many previously acceptable roles. Self-respect is sometimes mentioned as a reason for not wanting to take some types of work, once again pointing to an unhealthy sense of entitlement and an unfair lack of value placed on some areas of work. This may change as people's personal economic situations change and if currently low-value jobs begin to attract a higher value.

At the other end of the continuum, when people are comfortably off, they are increasingly likely to expect more alongside their pay and are sometimes prepared to take pay cuts as long as they can access other forms of compensation from employers that enrich their life in ways that make sense to them. People will also leave jobs and move to new employment in order to access the benefits that they value.

The bottom line is that pay still matters but it is not enough. What matters more to people now are their personal aspirations, things like self-development, well-being, causes that people identify with; even living where they want to. Flexibility in terms of working hours and where people work from is huge for people. Plenty of people will only search for jobs that meet their flexibility needs. Employees are prioritizing what they want to do in their wider lives, heavily influenced by their tribe and peers, to the extent that they are no longer as keen to move up the hierarchy at any cost to their lifestyle or health. Faced with this new reality, employers are hitting succession strategy hurdles.

Workers or all ages in permanent roles (and also a high proportion of workers in temporary roles) are interested in the culture of their employers and prospective employers. However, what they actually consider as important organizational factors has changed dramatically. Many senior executives think that people value prestige factors such as company heritage or turnover, whereas many workers are now likely to feel more aligned to organizations that they see as less hierarchical, more flexible, and offering a range of benefits that make a personal difference to them. Traditionally, elite organizations may have offered swanky offices, gym membership on-site, and free food. Today's workforce is more likely to rate a culture that offers flexible well-being packages, self-development funding, and tickets to a range of entertainment. More than anything, however, they value flexibility and a management style that creates an effective high-trust environment.

If organizations don't deliver on expectations, people will just move on. In the past, moving around too much was considered a no-no. Now it is the people who have stayed a long time with one employer who sometimes find themselves having to explain why. Dynamism is associated with flexibility, increasingly the most important skill needed both at work and outside of work. Companies have to develop radically different hiring strategies to meet the needs of prospective employees who don't want to spend much time applying for new roles.

Perhaps less motivated by promotional opportunities than in previous generations, people need stronger reasons to work hard rather than just to get by. In the new work environment, informal standards are being set by employees not employers. Whereas people tolerated pretty soul-destroying work realities "back in the day," there are now new work expectations that dictate whether people stay or go. One is the expectation of flexibility; another is being appreciated; and the third, a bit of a dark horse that has risen in importance very rapidly, is the absence of the absolute role-killer: boredom. For much of today's professional workforce, there is nothing less desirable than a boring job. With "experiences" being the currency of today, wasting time being bored is a very strong negative indicator and a legitimate reason for people to leave a given role.

On the flip side, people increasingly want variety in their work. Gone are the days when people were OK with being constrained by their job title. Now they want to have the opportunity to be themselves—using their skills in different ways and with different teams. Previously reserved for prestige training schemes, the opportunity to learn about different aspects of a business and dynamically change one's input into different areas of work could tick many boxes for today's low-boredom threshold workers.

Of course, not all jobs can be highly stimulating. In the past, many boring jobs were tolerated because of societal norms putting more value on job security and the absence of alternatives. A great many repetitive jobs have now been automated, but we are a long way from removing boredom from the workplace. In today's world, people are starting to expect a pay premium or some other type of sweetener for doing jobs that others don't want to do. People may expect flexibility in working arrangements to enable them to fit boring work around their lives, and they may even be looking to employers to make work less boring by offering development opportunities or designing roles to incorporate more variety, perhaps in consultation with them.

The background of people working, certainly at the frontline or entry-level jobs, has changed recently, becoming far less uniform and predictable in recent years. Whereas in the past, people working in call-centers or warehouses might have been uniformly less-well educated and low-skilled, people have reset their priorities so this no longer applies. During Covid, some people at more senior levels decided to leave (or were forced to leave) their existing work. Many returned to the workforce but not to the sector or at the level that they had previously held, deciding to downsize their jobs in favor of a lifestyle choice to have more free time or less stress. For many people, this meant changing to a job that offered flexible, remote working.

This has resulted in a far more diverse group of lower-end workers in some organizations than might have been the case in the past. Previously, more senior people who may be theoretically overskilled for roles are now working alongside people with more traditional backgrounds. People will have had very different prior experience, and therefore, individuals may have very different expectations of relationships with colleagues and managers and the culture of a working group. Failing to understand this new reality when thinking about the way that teams (whether remote or not) are managed may lead to frustration and misunderstandings between team members.

Although the desire for flexibility is one of the most powerful new "facts on the ground," you can see that it is part of a complex picture of changed lives and expectations. In the UK, we have a diverse workforce with a multitude of origins and lifestyles. Flexibility to prioritize what matters within different cultural lifestyles is an increasingly important issue. Though we have a long way to go on issues of gender equality, things have improved a great deal, and people's family arrangements reflect a society where people live and work in a complex tapestry of comings and goings for both women and men. These fluid realities need flexible working arrangements.

Organizations now accept that in order to operate with a viable work-force, they have to offer flexible working, otherwise they will not have the staff to operate. There are already severe labor shortages in several key industries in the UK (hospitality, road haulage, and the travel industry, for example) caused by people leaving these sectors during Covid and not being attracted back because the world and the lifestyles the workers wanted had changed in the interim.

As we are taking a reality check, it is important for balance to separate out what people want and the actual impact of remote work on them. Remote working arrangements may practically solve problems for people in terms of giving them the flexibility to reconfigure their life priorities but, badly thought out and managed, it can in reality be suboptimal or even harmful.

Whether commercial or public, organizations operate within difficult and very fast-moving social and economic conditions that dictate how they behave and constrain their choices. Different working arrangements have to make sense from many different respects, not just because workers want them. If it is the case that work-at-home policies are a begrudging reaction to a tighter labor market, without assessing the impact on business, or without the genuine commitment of senior managers, then the benefits of remote working are not likely to materialize for that organization.

Equally, if organizations just work out that they can save money by changing to remote work for the majority of their staff and implement it solely on this basis, without considering the complexity (and cost) of managing people in a way that delivers ongoing performance gains, they will be setting themselves up for serious problems. Establishing remote working as solely a cost-cutting exercise is likely to result in management that is not fit for purpose for the new working environment and which could compromise staff well-being. Without thinking strategically about long term remote working arrangements, the transfer into remote working could be fraught with problems. Without considering how people actually behave with new working arrangements, organizations can be disappointed by outcomes and lurch around looking for workarounds to problems that should have been considered at the start.

People are demanding work setups at present that they think will be an improvement over more traditional arrangement. After the initial novelty of remote work lifted productivity, people may have settled in to a more relaxed way of working and fear having to raise their game if they return to an office. People may have become used to working on their own and have forgotten the positives of interacting with others. It is frequently reported by people who delve back into face-to-face work for a short period after a lengthy spell of remote working that they immediately feel "lighter" and energized by human company.

Working remotely can be argued to take the specific identity of a career away. The normal trappings of working in a glamorous industry, or a learned institution, or a cutting edge innovatory start-up don't surround you when you are sitting at your dining room table. For people who have long-aspired to join companies in specific fields or because of the kudos associated with working in a certain location, or mixing in particular environments, working remotely takes away some of that childhood dream motivation attached to a particular career. It is plain to see that this sense of isolation from the "feel" of an industry is most concerning as it affects young people and people new to an industry.

All of the negatives that are associated with working extensively over screens rather than in-person, as discussed earlier in this book, are likely to be risks in a remote work environment. So the question becomes how can remote work be properly designed and managed for the benefit of both organizations and workers?

The need for proper strategic thinking is underlined by the very fragile uncertainty that now exists. Inflation is higher than at any point in decades, people are naturally worried about their finances, and some who may have moved location during lockdowns are perhaps considering whether they have taken the right decision. It may seem also that the news is full of issues that are impacting negatively on the economy and security. All of these factors make it extremely important for organizations to think carefully about how they maintain remote working as part of their working arrangements. Otherwise, remote work could be imagined to be more utopian than it actually is, both for organizations and workers.

Work is a major source of security for people. The mid-21st century is shaping up to be one of the most unstable times in recent history. Employers will inevitably need to do a lot to reduce the impact of instability on the economy and upon people's lives by providing job security and support. The appreciation of this environment of anxiety in workers' lives and the taking of reasonable efforts to reduce it will include the provision of remote work opportunities.

Making Decisions About Remote-Work Options

Before the day-to-day management of remote or hybrid working, decisions need to be taken about what model to actually use. A discussion about remote working could take place as a result of a strategic or human resources review. By scanning the skies in their particular work sector, senior managers and business analysts will pick up the potential for cost savings and other economic impacts. It is likely to be human-resources teams who will be at the front line of the debate with board members as they see first-hand whether people are applying for and accepting roles that are on-site, hybrid, or remote, and what conditions of employment they are trying to negotiate for themselves. If people are insisting on at least hybrid (if not fully remote) work, then Human Resources will be very keen to find a way forward to prevent vacancies remaining unfilled. The process for deciding to go or stay hybrid (or fully remote) should be an opportunity to look at improving the way that the organization works in general.

The objective is then to consider cost savings alongside making the organization less hierarchical and silo-oriented and more responsive to change, cross-functionality, promoting initiative and self-management together with effective new ways of managing potentially disparate teams. This may involve a full strategic review of the business or a more focused review of how remote working will contribute to these agendas.

The corporate review will, of course, consider not only employee convenience or cost considerations but fundamentally how customers should be served. Quality of service must be prioritized in business decisions. A discussion about remote work can prompt innovation in how services are delivered. For example, the availability of remote colleagues at different times of the day can enable organizations to offer flexible online options in industries that previously only offered face-to-face services such as teaching or counselling. This opportunity however also brings the temptation to offer services that are lower in quality and less effective than their face-to-face versions. Care should be taken to ensure that what organizations offer is not made inferior by a move to remote work.

Taking education as an example, Richards Hil's *Whackademia* shared concerns from anonymous contributors about learning being delivered via technology, creating what is described as a "formulaic, googlized, dumbed down education."[1] This study is from some years ago, but the concerns are still there and they have been joined by the loud voice of student discontent about enforced online learning as a result of the COVID-19 pandemic. The quality and experience of face-to-face learning are consistently felt to be better than online. There are fears (as in other sectors) that a two-tier system will emerge, with the privileged and higher-paying accessing services delivered by people, while others have no choice than to access services online only.

Truly flexible working hours will still need to respect the need for real-time interaction, either with customers or with colleagues or with both. If customers are mainly available during regular working hours, it will not be appropriate for staff who need to engage live with them to do the majority of their work "out-of-hours"; the flipside is that staff can be employed remotely in different time-zones to offer round the clock availability if required.

One of the biggest questions facing an organization will be should we go fully remote or hybrid. Of course, this depends. I've previously high-lighted the many problems potentially associated with working remotely, many of which relate to isolation and well-being but also include the dif-ficulty for organizations to maintain an effective corporate culture when having limited physical presence in people's lives. Common sense tells us that from a well-being point of view that hybrid is probably the best model for most organizations, enabling many of the cultural changes and efficiency savings of remote work, while offering a way to retain face-to-face contact with colleagues, so addressing some well-being, teamwork, and communications issues. By providing a physical group workplace, the employer also bears some additional costs of employment, rather than the

---

[1] www.newsouthbooks.com.au/books/whackademia_an-insiders-account-of-the-troubled-university/.

onus being on the worker to provide a place of work. This can be a big sign of long-term commitment to its workers by an organization.

Fully remote working is at one end of a continuum, with totally on-site work being at the other. Fully remote working allows people to log-in and work from anywhere with an Internet connection. (Theoretically, you could work remotely without being online and even mail in your work but, realistically, remote work is conducted online.) This brings the most gain in terms of complete flexibility of location and with it freedom from commuting. It also means that you don't have to work at all in a physical environment that you might not like or in the physical presence of people you don't want to be with. Further benefits include potentially being able to work at any time rather than keeping set working hours and, of course, the flexibility to fit remote work around other elements of your life such as child care or even another job.

Some types of work are particularly amenable to the totally remote work setup. IT and other jobs where people spend most of their time at a computer screen and already conduct meetings and chats online are considered particularly suitable. IT professionals are used to collaborating online because of the geographically dispersed nature of different parts of the team; they were already effectively working in a remote way but housed within offices before the advent of mass remote work. Temporary contracts for work which is output-based and can be delivered online (such as routine administration) are other examples where remote work can bring together a rapid response workforce to deliver the goods.

Working entirely remotely offers the huge opportunity to work with colleagues and customers across the globe. This means that we can have a deeper insight into the way that people work when living in different cultures. This global teamwork can do much to create greater understanding of the strengths of colleagues and the commitment to shared goals. This may be a contributory factor in bigger aspirations of reducing stereotyping about ethnicity, faith, or culture. Working with someone remotely creates a true shared and neutral experience where factors such as gender and age should not feature. Introducing different groups of people remotely who have not traditionally worked together is the first stage to breaking down some of these stereotypes. Remote working can be featured in a complete program of activity for international work, which could include sabbaticals where people could work directly and in-person with colleagues in other locations.

From an organizational perspective, fully remote work can mean dispensing with expensive office premises, saving large amounts of money that would have been spent on rent, utilities, and other related costs such as company cars. People can be recruited from a wider and deeper pool of labor, possibly from anywhere in the world and jobs can be refilled with ease as generally there is a ready labor-force wanting to work fully remotely. People may even be willing to work for less pay. In a high-trust environment, people can be left to "get on with things" rather than being closely supervised, perhaps saving on management costs. Some organizations may see benefits in not having to deal with the "people issues" that inevitably go hand-in-hand with people working together in-person.

As discussed, going remote can also highlight how superfluous some people are within the hierarchy. People can show that they need less management, and managers can also show that they can do some of the work of others in the team. Identifying these redundant positions is part of the new landscape of working. Before dispensing with roles, questions need to be asked about the general assumptions that were made in the past that led to "zombie" roles and whether improved remote performance is down to the person concerned being especially able to take on the work of subordinates or peers without compromising their own work, or whether improvement is more generally transferable.

So the upsides related to totally remote working are generally about cost and convenience for organizations. For workers, the benefits are overwhelmingly about convenience (flexibility) and to a lesser extent being away from aspects of working life that they don't like (commuting, micromanagement, and friction with colleagues).

When work is fully remote though, it does come with all of the potential problems that I have highlighted earlier: loneliness and isolation and the absence of a sense of work community. In extreme cases, there is even the potential to gradually become more disassociated from the outside world. Remote communications, though providing a functional way to communicate, also bring many problems from misunderstandings to the need for validation and concentration issues. Working fully remotely also brings the most risk of losing touch with healthy norms of work including self-care issues such as not working to burn out, poor diet, and exercise. For an organization, improperly managing remote work can lead to avoidable harm to workers and reputation damage. It can also mean that some employees abuse the remote work system to "shirk" rather than work. Poor management may result in previously motivated workers ending up abandoning trying to work effectively and just cruising—delivering the minimum that is expected of them rather than risking doing the wrong thing.

Practically, purely remote work just isn't an option for a large number of jobs; some roles need at least some attendance at a specific location. For example, a pharmacist may spend some of their time at a workplace checking drugs and sometime liaising online with patients or doing administration.

Benefits of Hybrid Working

Hybrid working is a compromise that could square the circle between the increasing demand for flexibility in work options from staff, the well-being benefits afforded by working in-person with others, and the strongly held beliefs of people on both sides of the remote working argument: those who feel that people should return fully to the office and those who feel that working from home is the answer. Organizations that offer a hybrid work model often offer it in conjunction with a 100 percent work-in-office alternative, so for those people who want or need to be on work premises, there is an option to do so.

Hybrid usually means a number of days a week in an office and the rest at home—typically two or three days in an office. The actual days could be self-selected or dictated by managers and, in very flexible arrangements, could vary from week to week—the version involving the most trust and coordination complexity. Another variation is split-week (when different teams or functions attend on different days of the week). There is also a model of hybrid working where some workers always work in an office, while another group of workers do the same work remotely; however, this model is quite rare, especially since, given the choice, most people would rather work totally remotely over being totally office-based. More unusual are arrangements where people work totally remotely but have in-office sessions less than once a week, say once a fortnight, month, or three months, which don't give the same hit of face-to-face interaction. In general then, hybrid involves at least some attendance at an organizational workplace in a set period of time.

As interest groups and individuals in society start to pivot into demanding work from home as part of the accepted way of working for their profession, so hybrid work is emerging almost as a given for higher-status work. We have reached a point at which if employers do not offer at least hybrid working as standard, people may decide to transition into another field or choose another profession or work-route at the training stage of their career. The expectation of more flexibility is creating a new hierarchy of work choices that could truly shake up the whole employment sector. The good news for hybrid work advocates is that it can bridge the gap between on-site and remote work. The infrastructure that we are familiar with is retained, and it enables an assessment of the most effective ways of working in different scenarios. For some organizations, it could even be the stepping stone toward more effective, totally remote working arrangements.

Hybrid work makes a lot of sense. With totally at the office or totally work from home setups, there is no room for flexibility; this is not so with hybrid work which can entail a number of different formats, which offer different degrees of flexibility. The aim of hybrid working is to give employees more freedom and work-life balance, while maintaining a better affinity with colleagues and the organization than totally remote work would allow for and keep productivity at a high level.

Working hybridly does tick the box for meeting colleagues face-to-face. The opportunity is there to mix with others in the kitchen and keep up with office gossip in the old school way. Importantly, we can also engage person to person with people working at different levels in the organization and wider sector. This allows us to develop an awareness of how things work career-wise, get the measure of other people and norms of behavior, and negotiate how to handle difficult aspects of work involving things like emotional intelligence and diplomacy. In hybrid working, we can talk about what we did out of work in the office and vice versa, so we should be able to get the benefits of job separation from work.

Hybrid working offers benefits for planning caring responsibilities for some people, as those with child care needs in a two-person household, for example, can alternate days working at home, enabling some flexibility with tasks like the school-run.

The ability to spend some days in the office and some days at home offers additional features that are not available in either an entirely remote or an entirely office-based work environment. A very common-sense adaptation that people make when moving into this work pattern is to segment workload into different types: the work-from-home type and the in-office type. So, people might naturally save research tasks for periods when working from home where they are less likely to be uninterrupted and keep tasks for in-office when they would value face-to-face input from colleagues. This self-selection offers people the chance to use their own initiative.

The old phrase "a change is as good as a rest" might apply also. When we are at home, we might realize that being in the office could be quite useful, for example, if we want to reach out and ask someone a difficult question. On the other hand, working in an office where people are talking around you while you are trying to concentrate (perhaps even to have meetings with remote colleagues on their laptops) may make you wish you were in your quiet home-office where you can just get on with the work and hear yourself think. Having an option to work in an alternative environment might offer the ideal balance for many people because of this contrast. When people work two separated days at an office and three at home, for example, it is never that long until you are going to be in the "other" environment.

Hybrid workplaces can specifically strengthen the elements that are weak in remote-working scenarios. As described, many of the problems with totally remote working are related to a vacuum of personal contact and bonding, leading to loneliness and isolation. The difficulty of communicating and collaborating effectively with co-workers is another danger area for remote workers. It is easy to see how sitting at a computer in an empty room all day can affect mental health and communicative skills negatively, especially over the medium- to long-term. By scheduling in at least a day a week in an office, hybrid workers can catch up on colleague contact and communication.

Hybrid working makes sense from an organizational culture perspective. The organization will still have the physical presence of premises as a feature of its commitment to and investment in its staff. It can provide facilities on-site that people value, such as gyms, eateries, and common rooms. Facilities can also be available to workers at any time, so that they can work at home during the day and use organizational facilities in the evening or weekend. These features greatly enhance the attractiveness of working for progressive and flexible organizations.

Being able to mix with colleagues and others face-to-face in group activities ensures that people can still make a personal impression. Networking, delivering important presentations, and the like are all possible on days reserved for group activities. It is important that these sorts of activities emphasize the value people add to the work and how people can work more effectively together and not just on personal alliances.

Another advantage of hybrid working is that of being able to learn from colleagues in-person (a major factor held up by executives as a reason to reject remote work). People can gain information online; however, there is no substitute for learning in-person with someone who is more experienced. When we have others to model our behavior on, we tend to make fewer mistakes and feel more confident in what we are doing. Learning can be blended though; working remotely and dovetailing this with in-person work with colleagues is a good balance.

Hybrid working may bring to bear some additional complications over and above purely remote working: it is not flaw-free. First, what model of hybrid working is best: one day per week remote, two days, three days, or a different variation? What is this based on and why? Is it the same for everyone or different from case to case? The hybrid split matters because this determines how work "feels" to people. If the vast majority of work is done "in-office," then working at home may be seen as a bit of a holiday day, when people focus on the (nonwork) things that they might need to be at home for and think of work as an afterthought. This "free day" mentality can cancel out the benefits of operating a hybrid work model by reducing a five-day week to a four-day one. There is also the issue of consistency: like any work policy, hybrid only works if it is offered fairly.

If some people in a team work at home for one day a week and others work at home three days a week, then accusations of favoritism could emerge (unless decided through personal choice). If some people are compelled to work on particular days, while others can pick and choose, this is likely to lead to animosity and discontent. Even if everyone has the same working pattern, relatively minor things such as Bank Holiday arrangements and seating plans can cause work angst.

Anyone who has worked in a hybrid office will also recognize the unfortunate scenario of being stuck between two people both having online meetings. Despite the use of headphones, it can be very distracting to be among people all talking on video to colleagues who are working at home or in another office. If you find people having online conversations around you distracting (especially if you don't have noise cancelling headphones), you may wish for totally remote working, or at least wish that people could go into an office to have a meeting. With the aim being to make working attractive both on remote and in office days, it is important to make office days as conducive to work as possible, otherwise there will be a natural inclination to dread aspects of going in to work, whether this be difficulty concentrating with multiple conversations around you, or being required to arrive at a time that guarantees being caught up in rush hour going to work and back home.

Bridging the divide between remote workers and workers on-site is a challenge. It is important for people to feel that they are part of the same organization, rather than one group being "more important" than the other. Most times, the risk will be that people working from home feel less engaged than the office-based workers.

Hybrid work has the potential to erode the soft abuses that come with co-workers and middle managers. As face-to-face work is limited to possibly a minor part of the week, the optics-driven office-culture, with all its problems, is no longer as prevalent. This is good news for companies wanting to move away from ego-driven culture.

The task for work is to meet the expectations of a working population that demands access to remote or hybrid work, while ensuring that business interests are boosted rather than harmed by this. You would think that, given that hybrid working offers the best of both worlds, this would be the model of choice. However, for businesses to maintain a hybrid model rather than purely a remote one, they will have to continue to lease expensive office space, as well as provide IT kit for people to use during their at-home days. Purely on an economic basis, it may make more sense for business to maintain either an in-office scenario or a completely remote-working setup for groups of their staff.

On the whole, however, hybrid provides a good compromise between fully remote and fully on-site working arrangements, and I'd expect it to be the basis for future work arrangements in many cases.

The next sections will look at the practical process of moving to hybrid or remote working and the considerations needed.

Practical Management

Assessment

When managed effectively, remote working offers a high-trust, highly effective working environment. Within this, organizations can build and maintain a progressive and inclusive culture. The process of moving over to remote or hybrid working should not be done on a whim. It should follow a deliberate business analysis to look at the pros, cons, and risks. Here is a potential sequence:

- The first consideration is that of customers' need. It is foolhardy to try and squeeze services into remote delivery if this will result in a much inferior customer experience. Other services or tasks without direct customer contact may be more suitable.
- How technically easy or difficult is it to do the job online? Can the role be undertaken without reference to other people most of the time? If collaboration is needed, how possible is this using technology? Do people need to work across geographies (which working remotely may facilitate)?
- How fair is it that the role is offered remotely? Is the role only being offered remotely because it is a perk expected by someone with power in the organization? Are all roles properly assessed or is it assumed that some people will get what they want? Remote working strategies that appear based on hierarchies rather than logic have the potential to be controversial and divisive.
- What will be the impact of remote work on the worker? This is a huge deal and really needs proper thought before any role becomes fully remote. There are a great many variables that can come into play and considerations that need to be made to minimize any negative impact. For example:

Is the work temporary work or long-term? Temporary work to cover a specific project, for example, is likely to have set deliverables and can theoretically be more tightly structured than a permanent role.

Are the risks of remote working recognized and have measures been implemented to minimize the potential harm of working remotely? This includes policies around health and safety, lone-working, use of technology, and regular worker psychological health appraisal and feedback.

Is effective management support available and for remote work in general and for specific roles?

Effective management is a critical element that will be explored in detail in the next section of the book. Support and proper management need to be detailed before remote working is implemented. This needs to cover everything from providing the correct equipment to detailing how work culture will be reinforced and people developed throughout their time working for an organization. This is the bit that organizations frequently mess up, mainly because it is assumed that individual managers will be able to manage as they did when work was not remote: this is incorrect.

For very particular scenarios, such as where people work on short-term contracts or have plenty of human connection in other areas of their lives and where remote management and support have been proved to be good both in terms of worker well-being and productivity, totally remote working may be assessed as being an optimum arrangement. Creating a high-trust environment must be the aim in a remote-only situation.

Other scenarios may point to the desirability of totally remote working from an organizational perspective—highly technical work needing little collaboration, or project teams which are geographically dispersed globally, for example. Cost savings may show the totally remote working model to be a no-brainer, especially as organizations have to cut costs to maintain margins and profitability. Although there may be overwhelming logic in making these roles totally remote, much thought and effort should be put into getting the expectations and management of these roles absolutely sorted before they start so that people thrive in these roles without being adversely affected by the negatives that all-remote working can bring.

Only those roles that fit within the scope of being cost-effective, customer-acceptable, worker-achievable, and manageable should be considered for being totally remote and there should be a comprehensive assessment of how employee welfare can be maintained and improved when working remotely. If this can be achieved, then remote working can result in high-trust, culturally diverse, and productive teams with a high level of maturity and flexibility.

However, most people accept that in a world with increasingly fragmented communities and diminishing in-person contact, actually being within workplaces with other people is an important source of human contact, contributing to well-being in the background. Even if we begrudge being in the company of workmates sometimes, it is generally healthier to have company at work. The harmful effects of totally remote working can be insidious, only becoming obvious when we get together with others in on-site work or even in a social environment where we can feel the difference that real human company makes when compared to doing everything via a screen. The novelty of all-remote working can also quickly wear off, leaving managers with the headache of trying to figure out how to turn things around.

Because the all-remote working model is at the extreme end of the work environment continuum and has the risks associate that I've described, in most cases, a remote-hybrid model may provide a better option. Hybrid working allows for real human interaction and potentially better well-being outcomes for workers. In many ways, being "in the room" with colleagues, whether peer or management, fosters commitment and a sense of work identity that is far harder to create online-only.

Hybrid working is a model that seems to offer the best of both worlds: the convenience and flexibility of remote work plus the human-contact and comprehension advantages of face-to-face working. Saying that, organizing hybrid working across an organization, or even in one team, is far from easy and many managerial issues associated with remote-only working still apply to hybrid working.

Next, I'll be looking at how remote and hybrid work can be managed successfully for the benefit of all. The best way to think about this is to go right back to first principles and consider how people behave and respond in the circumstances defined by remote and hybrid work. Management of flexible working models is really about good management in general, about enabling people to work on-task, with others and with a high degree of self-reliance. By thinking creatively and pragmatically about managing people in new ways, organizations can become strong, fit for purpose, and highly regarded workplaces.

Practical Management

Process

There is no blueprint for how to manage people working remotely, just as there is no set way to manage people in general. Every industry, organization, and team is different, and it is the skill of management to tailor itself to draw the best from individuals and teams in increasingly challenging times.

Whether entirely remote or a combination of remote and on-site, there will need to be a great deal of thought put into how to put into place the elements that ensure that teams understand the expectations made of them and produce the work that they need to, that people understand how to work together, and most importantly, feel included and motivated within the team. There is a school of thought that says that no real adjustment should be made to the way we think about remote workers—they are, after all just doing a job, as they would be if they were on-site. This perspective does not appreciate that remote workers often have specific motivations and that we are all programmed to behave differently when we work and interact online rather than in person. To concentrate on the procedural issues surrounding remote work, while ignoring the behavioral issues leaves the door open for problems. When people are working within an environment that depends more on trust than ever before, it is the way that people feel that dictates whether remote working will be a success, or will result in apathy, or even be harmful to the individual worker and the organization.

Remote working can be applied to all manner of different working contexts, from teams doing basic admin to teams working out complex solutions, creative teams to technical teams; academics to call-center staff. Given the diversity of working scenarios, it is an organizational-level responsibility to explore how best to manage remote work in different contexts.

Common sense can be drawn upon to preempt some of the key themes for groups: administrative workers may have a very clear idea of the process and outputs required. The biggest issue for this group may be isolation and feeling sidelined, for project teams, the biggest issue may be effective communication between different team groups, and for contact-center workers, the main issue can be feeling connected to the rest of the team and the wider organization.

If specific sections of an organization institute remote working and others remain on-site, this can reinforce silo working and an "us and them" mentality unless the basis for the split makes sense for everyone—and that depends on the decisions about remote working being shared and discussed openly. Any suspicion of randomness or unfairness in decisions about where people work is likely to be rightly disputed and goodwill withdrawn: it is very important that decisions are fair and transparent and communication is inclusive and open.

People on the whole no longer prioritize being with the same employer long term; they are more likely to want to develop new skills or exhibit their personality at work (be themselves). By acknowledging people's motivations and interests and aligning them with organizational goals, managers are likely to create personal and corporate loyalty. People increasingly see work as an opportunity to express their personality and as one element of their life, alongside many others that may take priority. Understanding the goals and motivations of people in this light requires a fresh approach that is open about work being able to add value to life more holistically.

Within departments and teams, attention needs to be devoted to how to shape how work on the ground is best structured, conducted, and delivered remotely and also to be able to predict and preempt any problems at a practical level. This will require an iterative approach, changing as people settle in to their new working routines and can feedback on what is working well and what could be improved.

Remote working holds out hope for the age-old problem (especially for larger organizations) of working in silos. Interactive applications exist to support teamwork both across and between organizations. The ability to communicate, share knowledge, and work on projects together online is undeniably useful; however, the added benefits of people working physically together, actually in the same room, need to be considered also.

In summary, there are a great many permutations of work, people employed, management-style, organizational culture, and external factors bringing to bear on how best to design, implement, and manage remote working. Each scenario will be different but there are some common-sense considerations that can be applied to make remote working a success.

Bring Structure

Remote working needs a strong structure. Without people knowing what they are doing, by when and with whom, remote work has the potential to be a confused and potentially short-lived experiment for an organization. It shouldn't just be assumed that people can deliver exactly the same as with on-site working without checking this out via business analysis and gap identification. This will involve a back-to-basics exercise of looking at everything that is required and practically how this will work with people working remotely. Managers need to consider what their team members will deliver and the steps needed, stage by stage.

The reality of working remotely is that people can easily drift into spending time on "activities" (like Internet research) and lose focus on goals. Of course, this can happen with on-site work also; however, it is all too easy to feel that being logged-on equates to being productive when working online in isolation from others. There are many remote distractions that we can easily feel equate to work, when they don't take us any closer to our goals. This "drift" also applies to on-site work and this is why an overall review of tasks can sharpen up expectations generally; however, being remote means that the range of distractions becomes far greater.

To make remote work more focused, it is better to state progress toward outcomes in terms of outputs rather than activities. This will obviously work well when people are doing routine tasks such as administration remotely, but it is also useful for more complex work areas so people can tie activities to specific outputs and outcomes that are needed within set time frames.

The process of deciding on outputs and outcomes and how people's time will be structured to achieve these while working online also enable other improvements. Going through the steps can identify wasted energy in processes that may not have been noticed (sometimes for a very long

time) in the past. It could be that moving to remote work can eliminate steps that were necessary with on-site ways of achieving the same
outcomes. In some cases, waste processes may exist that are not needed
wherever people are working, but this has not previously been noticed.
In routine processes, this can be as easy as working out that documents
don't have to be sent to another person to be passed on, if they can be
passed on directly. Other commonly redundant steps include unnecessary
meetings, involving people out of politeness and overlong waiting periods for feedback when fairly immediate feedback is possible. It is at this
stage that it may become obvious that some roles are not needed or can
be restructured to add more value. It may also become clear where there
are no safety nets in place, for example, if key people can't be accessed or
if technology fails.

Bringing structure to a remote working team in terms of the basics of
when people will be working, with whom they will be working, and what
they need to deliver gives a good foundation for day to day remote work.

Working remotely can mean that we can feel remote from the purpose
of the organization itself, so finding ways to help each person identify
with this is important. As part of this remote work planning exercise,
managers need to home in on the task allocation in the team. The outcomes need to be clear, and even more so than when people work on-site,
people need to know how their work fits in with everyone else's. This is
because people will not necessarily be reminded of this by the cues that
exist when we work face-to-face with others, for example, sitting with a
team in an office where we can share progress by chatting across a desk.

Ways should be found to enable people to clearly understand what
their individual contribution is to group goals. It is essential to emphasis
how people work toward goals, as it can be easy to feel that an individual task is not connected to other work if this is not actively reinforced.
Crediting people properly for their contributions is an important task for
remote work managers. Joint projects and shared reporting can enable
people to feel connected to a larger team.

This should be emphasized at the start of any new piece of work and
reinforced by regularly having people share how their work has led to
outcomes in the bigger scheme of things and how they have helped other
team members. People can be introduced to allied areas of work to which

they can make a contribution. Remote methods offer new ways of engaging with other people's work, so, over time, people can associate in a potentially much deeper way with the organization. This will depend on people knowing what is going on more widely and feeling free to contribute, with the expectation that their contribution will be appreciated. Done right, this will reduce silo-working.

Remote working enables people to take the initiative in terms of developing enhanced scope for their work. For example, motivated people could become involved in international projects, or someone could more easily work on different stages of a piece of work if this is made more possible by working remotely.

Some Basic Practicalities

Remote work is generally conducted online. This means that the technology has to work (self-evident but a major cause of remote-working delay and frustration). Having expectations of people who can't work because of their tools not working is not OK. Messaging, video, and process technology should be fit for purpose and it should not be assumed that people automatically know how to use it—and people should not be assumed to be incompetent if they are slower at picking up the technology than others. People can easily be de-motivated because the technology is overkill.

Prompted by cues, employees can be guided through their daily work routines, theoretically leaving them free to concentrate on higher level tasks. However, these workflow tools are often not as intuitive to people as following old-fashioned person-to-person instructions, so it is best to reinforce them directly via discussion and demonstration. More basically, following online triggers can lead to people being conditioned to just stick to a set path (such as happens with satnav). This can remove the inclination to try anything different or to use one's own initiative and has the potential to leave people bored and de-humanized.

Routine is important. Having a regular daily stand-up will reinforce the discipline that can be a struggle for people working remotely. It is important that everyone talks in the stand-up, so that people stay comfortable with talking through progress. Using communication apps should also have some structure; even the little things such as having a photo on your avatar rather than just initials will humanize communication. Making sure that everyone contributes to a discussion means that no one is left out and forgotten.

Technological tools should not be the death of more traditional forms of communication. In particular, talking to people is important. Just because dropping messages is available as an option, it does not mean that we should do this if video is available. Keeping human contact is important.

Expectations and Boundaries

Remote work has the potential for people to be left floundering. People need to know what is expected of them, and boundaries need to be defined to avoid misunderstandings and wasted effort. This is particularly true in terms of the behavior of both managers and workers. It is easy to misunderstand what the boundaries are for use of time with remote work, so it is important that people are clear and can demonstrate their maturity about this. Being online does not mean that people need to be working every second; most people are very responsible about use of their time and pride themselves on being able to work in a trustworthy way. Of course, this is dependent on building an atmosphere where people are treated in a mature way within a high-trust environment.

Many tools show when people are online; it needs to be clear whether being online permits other people to video-call or not. If people are working out of hours, is it legitimate to contact them or should you assume that they are doing some work that needs no interruption? Labels can be used to indicate status, and it is important to check that everyone knows how to use them. Simple rules for remote work, such as responding within set time frames and not contacting people during some time periods, will help to reinforce boundaries and stop simple misunderstandings from escalating out of proportion.

Old-fashioned good manners are important. Ignoring people in calls and leaving messages unanswered are plain rude and often a throwback to the power games of on-site working. Such defensive behavior should be brought to the attention of managers and rooted out.

Remove Micromanagement

Traditional working environments supposedly have a built-in safety check to prevent workers running amok and abusing the system: they can be seen. However, this is an illusion since people have always managed to waste time in plain sight. Who hasn't seen colleagues spending all day chatting about nothing to do with work, or scrolling on their mobile for hours? The knowledge that people can behave like this, betraying the trust of the organization, can, in the minds of insecure managers, justify micromanagement: excessively close control of work.

Micromanagement is one of the most hated management behaviors and is a reason why people prefer the physical separation of remote work (no more having someone watching over your shoulder). Freeing people from micromanagement has not only been a huge relief for workers; in some cases, it has also enabled them to show just what they are capable of. Maintaining a higher trust environment is essential to the success of remote work if it is to be without the damaging (and hated) monitoring that some organizations have considered.

When remote working first burst onto the scene in Covid lockdowns, there was extreme fear that people would do the minimum and waste time; this was proved incorrect. People actually get on with their work diligently without close supervision from managers in most cases and certainly without micromanagement. The high-trust nature of the team depends on everyone respecting each other's integrity and demonstrating results. If a team is not well managed, this has the potential to slip into gaming this trust. Being transparent goes a long way to gaining respect, as does the willingness for others to be transparent. Simple things like sharing calendars and showing availability can be very reassuring.

Closer supervision is of course helpful when people first start. Indeed, it is very important for starters to be clear about their role and how they will be expected to communicate with other people and update the team. Starting a role is a critical time when people can "get it" and move forward, or feel lost and confused; the potential for the latter is higher when work is remote.

Communication and Support

People can be trusted to work remotely, but without clarity and boundaries, they may be likely to stray into time-wasting activities simply out of frustration, boredom, or confusion about what to do. Sharing expectations and discussing progress as a group help to strengthen understanding and trust.

In order to be effective, people need to know their objectives and how they will be able to achieve their tasks. This means that work-process and communications channels need to work effectively. In many roles, people need to closely coordinate with others and this needs good communication across a team. The way that people communicate should be agreed and transparent. Engaging regularly and predictably is the key to effective communication online as it reinforces expectations and also ensures that people are included; to this end, it is important to actually include people in the discussion, rather than people just being logged-on to a call.

Managers are the figureheads for support in the team. They are responsible for making sure that people feel included and supported in order to work effectively. They need to articulate the opportunities for people to contribute to progress, how people are held accountable, and how things will be handled if things go wrong.

Morale and motivation can be a problem in a remote work environment. It is down to managers to work out how to ensure people feel motivated. There is no one way to do this as teams are so different, but this will involve showcasing the importance of everyone in the team and designing specific opportunities to involve team members with work that they enjoy or are stretched by. This could be through involvement with other parts of organizational life.

New avenues of communication can open up opportunities for people wanting to learn or demonstrate their ability. Acknowledging and talking about people's individual aspirations and motivations (some of which are likely to be shared by others in the team) is a good way for managers to demonstrate their understanding and support for team members.

Unfairness of any kind is a real motivation-killer, so it is absolutely imperative that there is no favoritism. Remote workers need to know that they are not being treated less well than each other and also when compared to nonremote workers. There is plenty of potential for on-site workers to be unconsciously favored just because we tend to elevate people that we spend more time with. If there is a mix of remote and on-site personnel, it is important to be aware of this potential for unconscious bias.

Building Connections

This is another key aspiration for workers, one that is much more difficult to attain remotely. When we work physically among other people, we can network formally and informally. People get chatting; it is these interactions that can spark ideas, collaborations, and friendships, all of which are important to us in terms of work outcomes and self-esteem.

Connections are useful to progressing along a career path, and it is the limited opportunity to do this remotely that has prompted some leaders to urge people to return to on-site work so that they can benefit from rubbing shoulders with more experienced colleagues. Online learning, networking, and mentoring are possible, although it is not easy to build the familiarity and rapport that we need to nurture connections online. This is where regular opportunities created by managers to just get to know each other may help. There is no getting away from the fact that online networking however is NO substitute for actually being with people in-person—we are, after all, human beings and are programmed to respond to the charisma and warmth of others, qualities impossible to fully convey through a screen. At a more personal level, online channels of communication face many headwinds, from being concerned that we may be recorded against our will, to just feeling unnatural. As time goes on and we all adjust to undertaking the majority of work communication online, we could find this to be a lot easier.

It is important that spaces are created for remote-only workers to be able to learn from colleagues and contribute in ways that recognize their extra commitment to, and interest in, the organization. These need not be traditional networking formats, although virtual social engagements could play a part. Online games and challenges are great ways of enabling remote workers to show off their skills and rapport with other colleagues—this could be a massively growing area of activity within business.

It could be said that building connections has traditionally been unfair to people who don't share the right background to impress some of the big guns in many sectors. Perhaps, moving building connections at least partly online does enable people to build work relationships in a way that provides a more level platform.

Another key question in the new remote-only world is about corporate culture. How can organizations maintain a culture without people physically mixing in offices and benefitting from the perks of on-site gyms, restaurants, and other features? The answer is very pragmatic: improve what you offer outside the office and learn from great online-only retailers and other businesses about what makes a business develop an identity without a physical presence or heritage. Valuing your staff and customers by asking them what *they* feel will add value to their lives—from local gym membership to vouchers for fuel bills will identify organizations as employers who understand and value their workers. Online-only retailers spend a lot of time and money engaging with customers and colleagues to make them feel personally valued and included.

Working remotely has the potential to more easily accommodate different personalities, the most sticky diversity issue around and one that is not really mentioned but has a profound effect on team dynamics and performance. It is obvious that some types of personality do better than others in traditional in-person working environments: more extrovert people make themselves known more easily for example, and this visibility in itself can lead to better opportunities for them. Remote working can flatten this advantage by enabling people to input in different ways that puts less emphasis on having the strongest physical presence.

The onus is on managers to find ways to make personality differences a strength in remote working, for example, by offering people an opportunity to get involved with work outside their immediate area or on stand-alone projects drawing on their own interests and skills. Some people will prove naturally adept at finding creative ways to work remotely, and this should be encouraged. Remote work is likely to be the making of a hidden group of people who were formerly underappreciated in the on-site environment.

Danger Signs

There is a blueprint for establishing the ground rules for remote working in terms of structure, expectations, teamwork, and connections. Good managers can set up remote work in a purposeful way with the tools needed to make it work. They can ensure that staff are properly included via remote means and encouraged to extend their connections with others across the organization and further afield. Freed from the grind of commuting and micromanagement, people have an opportunity to shine on a more level-playing field, away from the biases and ego-based politics of the physical workplace.

This is not the whole picture, of course. Working totally remotely carries intrinsic risks linked to our primitive psychological tendencies and resultant behavior. Just giving people the tools to do the job remotely does not mean that they will be unscathed by working in this way as far as the impact on their performance and well-being over the medium and long term. I would like to turn now to thinking again about some of the red flags to be aware of.

People report a need and preference to be together to prevent isolation. Being at work involves far more than getting work done, the social payback for most of us is being with people and working toward a common goal. It is sobering to think that most organizations still have, hidden in their batches of compliance documents and health and safety policies, documents outlining a policy for lone working. These were written in the days before remote working as we now know it. It seems illogical that the advice given to avoid lone working because of its negative outcomes can be withdrawn almost overnight, without considerable safeguards being implemented.

Lone working has long been recognized as a risk to employees in terms of the physical danger of being assaulted while working alone in an office and also of the problems associated with being segregated and working in an isolated way. These policies need revisiting in the era of widespread lone working, since both areas of risk still exist; indeed, it may be far more likely that people are assaulted at home by people that they know than by strangers at an office. Management has a responsibility to recognize the risks of remote working arrangements and mitigate them.

What's more, we don't notice changes in well-being because we are not physically with people, we just see them over a screen, so it is very hard to tell whether someone is not as "well" as we are used to seeing them. Poor mental health can often be left unnoticed and untreated for far longer in a remote setting.

Overload

People working remotely can work in an always-on, work-from-anywhere environment. Even if your employer has a well-being-focused human resources policy, dedicated to ensuring your health and welfare, the *potential* to carry on working will still be there. This could really mess up your work-life balance. The culture of our hyperconnected society steers us toward continually doing something online, and for some people, this will mean they feel obliged to work into their own time. This carries the risk of health and welfare problems associated with never really switching off. Recovery time away from work completely is a vital part of recuperation and health.

Just as we are guided by social media to click on links, it can also be tempting to delve deeper and deeper into issues with limited comprehension of when to stop, or what is relevant. It may be difficult to keep abreast of what is an important issue or opportunity to collaborate and what is just noise online. It is not just information overload that causes us stress, factors such as worry about the security of our data, our need for instantaneous validation, and our constant online connection with others can all bring us down with a crash, or wear us down until we mentally switch off.

It is hard to resist the drive to open more tabs or follow breadcrumbs leading nowhere. Policies need to emphasize that having loads on the go does not equate to being a better worker. Concentration and focus should be valued, and higher-level tasks made available for colleagues rather than just the availability of more of the same. A strong message is needed that producing results is the goal: not looking busy.

Totally remote working can become one long round of work activities from a desk. It is not really like working within an office or other workplace at all, where many of us will do some work, then walk over and chat to a colleague, then go and sort something out with another team and so on. Online we tend not to leave any space between meetings and blocked out production time. This can raise productivity but it does nothing for our well-being. The endless barrage of back-to-back tasks does not include the gaps we need for recuperation in between tasks. It is advisable to limit days without gaps or build in recovery time.

Motivation and Trust

The new connected culture that is being presented is one of a shift toward more flexible and collaborative ways of working, rather than command and control. This works for highly motivated, competent, and trustworthy teams and colleagues. The problem is that high levels of loyalty and motivation tend for many to go hand-in-hand with personal relationships and interaction at work, the very elements that might suffer if we are not careful. Away from environments where people are motivated enough to self-manage online working, employers may come across people trying to "game" systems, especially if they already feel unfairly treated by changes in the wider economy.

Simultaneously, there is also an increased awareness among businesses of the perceived need to monitor their users and employees. With the risk that remote workers could be abusing the system, some managers feel that they need to employ a sophisticated array of checks and balances. Monitoring employees through IP address records, keyboard stroke counters, and even webcam surveillance has become commonplace in some environments. Working with this level of scrutiny can lead to a high level of stress, and a balance needs to be struck between identifying abuse and enabling worker autonomy. Automatic monitoring of this sort is low trust, arguably unethical and potentially illegal.

Separation of Work and Life

We all realize that problems at home can affect work, and problems at work can affect our home life. Imagine how much more exaggerated this may become if work happens at home. The separation of work and home life brings clarity and a sense of being able to adopt a more relaxed and personal identity outside of the work environment. Without the physical separation of going home from a place of work, we can find it difficult to transition out of work and into the vital period of recuperation away from work. Some people forced to work from home in Covid lockdowns, even started to miss the commute as this can be a period of transition from work identity to real identity.

Special training for all remote workers in spotting the warning signs of problems in one area of life negatively impacting on another may need to be available and counseling support made available.

Connections and Belonging

Ultimately, the biggest well-being problem for remote working is that we need human contact in order to make real connections with others. Human brains are wired to need regular social contact with other people, and neural connections are fired up by this contact.

Unfortunately for remote working, the connections with others that we need are strongest when we are physically around other people. Just being around others makes us feel a sense of belonging. This is reinforced when we have the chance conversations that pepper our day around an office, having ideas and catching up with others. Outwardly unproductive interactions are actually very, very important to forming the bonds that improve our working experience, particularly by preventing us from feeling isolated and by offering us support. This support is not just in terms of work but with personal issues too; how many times do we turn to a work colleague for a bit of reassurance with something going on outside work?

Talking face-to-face strengthens our communication skills. Work should enable people to shine and display their skills. The problem is that undue emphasis on technology may allow some people to conceal their weaknesses and others to disregard areas of strength. Finding a way to highlight personal talents is more difficult when we are all hiding behind a screen.

Face-to-face interactions are an important factor in reinforcing the organizational culture that we feel supports us and to which we belong.

When we all gather in a workplace, it is clear that we all work for our company. When we have online meetings, we could be working for any organization logged into a Teams or Zoom account. The whole sense of belonging is diminished.

When we start to lose our sense of belonging, it becomes a self-fulfilling prophesy as we can easily become less and less psychologically engaged with the organization and our colleagues. Remote working makes it relatively easy to slip into the shadows, especially if we work in a large team. Without an avatar, we can be reduced to just initials on a chat board; there are many places to hide in plain sight when it comes to remote work.

Remote working can quickly reduce the "existence" of people in a team and lead to a downward spiral of people not being expected to contribute, not contributing, feeling left out, and disengaging completely. This chain of events is difficult to see sometimes, and managers should implement measures to ensure that people contribute regularly and feel included. This is easier said than done.

****

In conclusion, for those people with the responsibility of ensuring that remote working is an asset rather than an expensive hindrance both to employee well-being and to business operations, there are some simple considerations to bear in mind.

First, the rationale for adopting particular digital systems must be clear. Remote working should be designed to be as easy to use as possible and it needs to make sense. Trying to accommodate more and more interfaces and options often does nothing more than leading to confusion and the likelihood that people will end up making mistakes. Organizations should conduct user research to see what people actually need and then undertake a pilot to show how any system is actually going to work in practice.

Good communication is essential. Remote working is no substitute for people actually getting together physically to work out problems, chew the fat, and get to know each other. However, online communication can be used not only for work but to get to knowing each other at a more personal level, in a less abstract way so that we get to understand how we can each draw upon strengths, avoid offending or pressuring people, and generally enjoy the process of working in a team. Spaces and times need to be built in to enable people to be together person to person. One-to-one interaction such as informal video calls should be encouraged.

Some employees will develop problems related to the relative isolation of remote work. Occupational health should provide lifestyle or medical advice and signposting at an early stage to help recovery and rehabilitation. Training should be available to spot the signs of deteriorating mental health when people work remotely.

Managing Hybrid Work

Perhaps, the best way of addressing the connection gap is by making remote work not entirely remote: by making it hybrid. I have talked about the decision to go hybrid earlier and will now discuss some practical elements in managing hybrid work. By using the hybrid working environment as not just a place to work but a way to redesign our working lives, we can address some of the problems that can and are impacting our well-being because of remote work.

In many cases, hybrid working solves many of the dilemmas posed by fully remote working, while not really adding many downsides apart from a loss of total freedom to work from anywhere, and therefore, organizations miss out on some potential employees who might only consider roles with total flexibility. Hybrid work also has the potential to retain bad office practices (ego-based management, etc.), but on the whole, it brings considerable benefits over a truly remote working environment.

The big advantage of hybrid working is that it enables people to mix in person, and so, people can benefit from the bonding that comes with working with other people. Features such as hanging around with people intrinsically make people feel a sense of belonging that can't be replicated online and is hard to articulate. You only really notice how good being with other people makes you feel when you are working on your own for a while. This both boosts performance and, importantly, well-being.

The hybrid model can be used to design individual learning plans that take into account when and how they are most productive. Remote working days can involve more flexibility, with longer breaks allowing people to break the cycle of back-to-back activity, while on-site days can be more structured and planned to allow best use of time that colleagues have to connect.

As a hybrid manager, you should be reinforcing the message that work is not just one meeting after another. Recovery and variety need to be built in. Indeed, I believe that there should be a limit on the number of back-to-back meetings people attend per day—whether remote or in-person. On-site days give the opportunity for a period of time spent with others that supports work. It sounds corny but finding a way to connect like we used to in common rooms can do wonders for well-being without too much effort. Thinking needs to move away from seeing this as "wasted" time and toward seeing it as time spent cultivating loyalty, connections, and well-being. Spending time like this also helps productivity by refreshing workers.

Since there is a combination of environments, extra effort is needed to make both remote and office-based time work well together, but, if you get it right, this will mean that your organization derives the benefits of remote working and minimizes the downsides. Theoretically, a hybrid workplace could operate on a completely remote basis if push came to shove and could be a staging post on the route to a totally remote setup. It is the combination of remote working plus on-site working that makes it an improvement over all remote working in most cases though.

A key issue with hybrid models is that typically some people will be working remotely at the same time as colleagues are in the office. This is because people will want to have different combinations of days working remotely. (Imposing specific days in an office is possible but why not give people a choice?) This means that there needs to be complete synergy between people working on-site on any day and their colleagues working at home. It entails online communication for discussions where remote colleagues are included and in-person discussions where people are physically present. If there is a mixture of remote and in-person attendees, it is important that remote attendees as far as possible don't feel like an afterthought on a screen that no one takes any notice of.

On-site days help us to experience the more complete mix of communication that we get when talking face-to-face with others. No one can genuinely say that talking remotely has the intensity that being with others in person has. Even the most charismatic person will come across as a bit flat, compared to their in-the-flesh self. This means that we can more easily zone out of communication that is via a screen and is why really important meetings should be in-person if possible. Working in a hybrid way gives organizations the opportunity to organize this.

There are many practical things to consider when going hybrid. Planning hybrid work schedules is not easy since managers have to take account of issues such as maximizing the opportunity of colleagues to meet in-person and ensuring that people have seating available within the office on any one day. All of these elements matter because when people are present in an office for a limited time, this time is special and should be used to maximum effect, not just in terms of work but also to reinforce connections and improve well-being. If people have to mess about trying to locate somewhere to sit when they arrive, this will make them feel second class and sidelined.

Personalization is an often forgotten element of working on-site. We like to make our space at work our own. Many people instinctively adorn their desks with photos and mascots. This is no coincidence as putting our personal stamp on things contributes greatly to a sense of security at work. Even just arranging your seating and computer in a way that suits you is a mark of ownership. This is important, and if space allows, it is beneficial to give people their own space or some other way of personalizing space, whether a physical space or online.

There is a debate about where managers should be in a hybrid work setup—in the office or remote? My view is that managers should, as a minimum, be available in-person to the extent that each person from the team can access them face-to-face at least once a week. They should also lead a connections activity for team members on the days that they are there and also for the whole team once a month. Managers should work remotely for some of the time in order to fully appreciate the remote working experience in terms of tools, technologies, and training for effective work. Importantly, managers should be trained to observe the dynamics of team members and recognize where people may be keen to have greater challenge or have more support when working remotely. They should take the lead in ensuring that people understand the collaborative nature of hybrid working, backing this up with activities during the in-person days.

Hybrid working must be fair. All workers must be working in a hybrid way on equal or near equal terms. Managers need to appreciate that having hybrid workers alongside colleagues who work entirely on-site may create a two-tier workforce with people who can't work remotely because of personal circumstances becoming resentful of those who can or those working significantly remotely feeling sidelined. There may be a temptation to favor people who are continually in the office just because they are more visible; this should be resisted.

Hybrid working arguably involves more adjustments for managers than moving to an all-remote setup. Hybrid work managers need to be good at reinforcing how things are done, from seating arrangements to rules about what still happens face-to-face rather than remotely. They need to be good at using technology and patient with those who might not be. Most of all, they need to be humble enough to give up some power when competent people successfully freestyle their work.

Managers may be leading people who have proved during lockdown that they don't need a manager's intervention to do the job. People may have learnt workarounds in order to be one step ahead of managers and use this to maximize the ease with which they reach their goals without supervision. This means that managers may need to cede some day-to-day control to workers who are able to work more autonomously by using technology and common sense. Alongside this, they will need to manage more strategically, creatively, and intuitively, thinking more about everything from scheduling to engagement, team development, and individual motivation. The on-site elements of management require creativity to enable people to form the connections that reinforce well-being. Emotional intelligence will be a far bigger element in the management of hybrid work.

I've talked about hybrid working as a work model where people go in to work at least once a week. There are other models out there that require people to get together less frequently, say once a month or so. This does not permit the usual connectivity that goes with working alongside colleagues on a weekly basis, and therefore, it does not build an effective sense of belonging and become an antidote to isolation. However, minimal hybrid working can rally people behind the organization, perhaps in order to commend and value work in an environment where people can relax, to reinforce corporate values, or bring people together to put faces to names. These regular, if infrequent, events can be augmented by remote communication building up to the in-person event, with people working together to represent their team and connections made during the event cemented in subsequent remote work and discussion.

This is a truly exciting and innovative time, both in terms of the technology and also in terms of the corporate and management behavior that needs to evolve parallel to the use of technology in business and the move to hybrid and remote working. Changes to the workplace, as a consequence of collaborative and social tools and the huge leap in functionality because of advances in computing and networking, bring the prospect of staff connecting and coordinating more effectively when working remotely. This needs proper assessment and management to avoid massive confusion and overload. Changes in behavior and psychology must be taken into account in this Brave New World of work; otherwise, we have a recipe for disaster—organizational frustration about why things aren't working in the way that has been anticipated, coupled with individual distress.

This is only the start for new working arrangements. In the next section, I look at some of the innovations that may be heading our way.

What the Future Holds for Work

Work is going to continue to be different because we are now different. Technology has changed the way that we think and behave, major world events have upset our equilibrium, and the only certainty around for the foreseeable future is that there will be a lot of uncertainty.

The trials and tribulations of the economy have left the labor force in a state of imbalance, with massive inequalities between the haves and the have-nots. Meanwhile, social media has played a massive part in amplifying people's expectations that they will achieve in life. Academic attainment has never been higher in terms of university degrees, feeding into the sense of entitlement that people feel. The reality is that many young people cannot afford to own their own home and continue to share accommodation until well into their 30s or longer. This has a knock-on effect in terms of remote working conditions for people who do not have a dedicated place to work from at home.

It is noteworthy that many remote jobs are more senior at present, perhaps reflecting the fact that affluent workers potentially have suitable remote working spaces available. If remote working is going to be accessible to all, where are people living in shared accommodation going to work from? Similarly, parents of small children may not have the calm environment needed to concentrate from home.

One answer may be the creation of networks of extremely localized work-hubs where people can log-in to work if they don't have the opportunity at home. However, if these are provided on a commercial basis, this may make the access to remote work divide worse. We are a very long way from realistic remote hub spaces being provided at scale by public authorities, such as within libraries.

So, remote working is really also about who has the prerequisites to do it. Might there come a time when employers contribute to things like child care or soundproofing to enable more of their workforce to work remotely? Theoretically yes. In practice though, people living in cramped, noisy accommodation at present are effectively disadvantaged or even ruled out of the remote work labor market. As a higher proportion of people who live in crowded accommodation are ethnic minorities, there could also be a race bias in who has the facilities to apply for remote work.

Covid seems a distant blur in the minds of many now. However, there is a new panic sweeping the globe that has its seeds in the financial crisis of 2007/2008—the global impact of pumping money into the global economy and high inflation and squeezed budgets leading to a cost of living crisis for people round the world. This has led to ongoing upheaval and, of course, the outcome is uncertain. What does seem clear is that the circumstances point to an ongoing worsening of mental health and the likelihood of panic about work and income. Under these conditions, it could well be that organizations attempt to cut costs by relinquishing expensive office premises in favor of remote work. As fuel prices make commuting an increasing cause of concern for workers, organizations may feel that they have a moral obligation to help alleviate the cost of living strain on employees by enabling them to work more at home in order to reduce commuter costs.

On the other hand, an increasing mood of desperation centered on jobs and incomes means that as time goes on, organizations may have the whip hand in dictating terms for workers, so some whose executives have a held a more traditionally office-first preference may use a potentially looser labor market to insist that employees are totally office-based. I feel that this is less likely than an increase in remote work however.

More people working remotely will have an impact on society. As was seen during lockdown, some people leapt at the chance to swap their urban home for somewhere in the middle of nowhere (with a good Internet connection). Property prices have risen in rural idylls and dropped in high housing-density areas; this trend may continue but may be tempered by the tendency for organizations to offer work on a hybrid rather than fully remote basis. The proportion of fully remote work is already well down on its peak during lockdown and continues to fall.

As people become increasingly reluctant to work on-site, this may lead to shortages of workers in sectors where there is no possibility of remote work. This may already be a factor in some industries; most noticeably, the airline industry where huge numbers of frontline workers were made redundant during Covid when air travel was massively restricted. When travel was opened up, airlines struggled to recruit people back into the sector as many had moved to roles with more flexibility and better perceived working conditions, including remote and more flexible work.

This begs the question of whether pay and other conditions will need to rise to continue to attract workers to some on-site work, where there may be continuing shortages of skilled workers. Skilled on-site roles (where people may also have the option to move into remote roles in other organizations) may have to offer premium rewards to continue to attract workers in future. If it becomes difficult to recruit people to frontline in-person-only roles such as manufacturing and social care, this could drive up wages in these roles also. As time has gone on, fewer people are willing to work in boring and low-paid work, with people at every level opting for work that enables them to maintain well-being and fits in with their overall life commitments wherever possible, leading to labor shortages in some areas and potentially surpluses in other areas.

This will lead to acceleration in the move to automate many routine and labor-intensive roles, from factory-line to construction. Robots, software automation, and Internet of things-connected devices will continue to take over the most boring and repetitive jobs and those jobs where they offer an improvement because of reductions in errors and improved quality and standardization. Not all manufacturing work will be automated however. High-value and complex processing could theoretically be made remote by delivering physical components to people's homes for hand-production or finishing. This would hark back to the days of skilled piece-work and would enable a subset of remote workers who do not sit at computers but actually make things. This model could include craftspeople, cooks, and technicians. In order to service this potentially growing area of remote work, the already massive home delivery and collection industry may grow even larger.

New work areas will appear, in particular in technology, but also in areas that have become greater priorities for people recently such as well-being and safety. Entertainment and culture could also become a growth area as people look to invest in their quality of life.

In the new economy, not all currently low paid and relatively unskilled roles will be equal. Although some jobs will disappear because of automation, this will not be the case for all low-paid work. Work which involves being face-to-face with other people that is impossible to deliver online, for example, nursing and social care, will continue to need people working on-site. These in-person jobs may attract a premium in pay at every level and also start to be viewed as higher status jobs. Indeed, nursing in particular has already begun to be seen as a more professional job since the pandemic, attracting far higher numbers of people who see it providing a clear career path and the flexibility to work anywhere in the world. Other caring roles which can only effectively be undertaken in-person may follow this lead and command greater status. Alongside this, there will be innovation that potentially makes some degree of remote work possible, for example, online nursing consultations and app-based monitoring. Although these initiatives may have their place, there is no real substitute for in-person care and support, particularly as we become more generally isolated in society.

As people move over to new business sectors which allow more flexible working arrangements, they will often need retraining. People will have to adjust to training for new skills far more frequently than in the past, as work requirements move rapidly with events such as greater automation and changes in expectations of what employees do. A flexible mind and willingness to change track in line with labor-market needs will define the survivors and beneficiaries of the new economic reality from the victims.

Using a battery of skills, workers of the future may have several jobs, whatever level they work at. They may even combine a more senior job with something more junior in order to experience a different working environment (remote or on-site), filling in the gap of needing more time at home or conversely wanting more human contact at work. People may also try out different jobs part-time and for short periods as an element of their career development. Organizations are increasingly realistic about diminishing loyalty from workers and will need to continually invest in activities to make staying with them attractive for staff.

For the less fortunate in the labor market, people may need to have several jobs at the same time in order to generate enough income to meet their needs. This may result in people moving around jobs with a low level of job security.

There is now a high level of cognitive dissonance between the aspirations of many workers and the reality of increasingly tough business conditions. There is a generation or more of people who, encouraged by social media, now feel entitled to higher status in their lives and "positive vibes only." This has led to a gap between expectations and reality. With a potentially tougher labor market to come, people may increasingly be asked to prove their worth, especially for the most interesting roles.

Many of these observations point to the emergence of more mental health challenges as people grapple with the speed of change and the gulf between what they want and what is available. The impact on mental health care provision is considerable and currently not being met. There is a real need to restore personal resilience and realism, countering some of the unrealistic and harmful visions of work and life held out over social media. Reality, for most of us, is that we can't automatically inhabit the work of our dreams: we have to work within the limits of the economy and society.

People will be made increasingly aware that real off-screen contact with others is essential for mental well-being, perhaps leading to "human company on prescription." Ironically, people could also be paid to provide human contact for people who feel very isolated. When so much of our life could be spent working in isolation and living in isolation and with real company being a premium activity, the future does start to look somewhat dystopian!

Another grim potential outcome of this cognitive dissonance is an extension of highly speculative get-rich-quick ideas that young people in particular may be attracted to. Already, many people have speculated on assets that they know very little or nothing about in the hope of gambling their way into the lifestyle they aspire to. There are plenty of people (especially on social media) willing to prop up the idea that speculative gambling makes sense. People following this track may define such investment as their work. Whatever direction the economy takes, I can't see this slowing down, given the vested interests, people chasing a solution to their finance issues and constant craving for the next big thing.

Remote working will enable more people across more industries to work from anywhere across the globe. This will open up access to greater cultural understanding as more people work with others of different races, faiths, and cultures. However, global working also brings some risks. Although some working practices, including remote working itself, may enhance some workers' lives, organizations may also import and borrow other cross-cultural practices that degrade working conditions such as fixed rather than permanent contracts or even lower wages.

It is not just remote work that provides a new model for how work is organized. There are currently experiments going on around the world looking at issues including Universal Basic Income and shortened working weeks for the same pay as for previously longer working hours. These experiments all hope to address the dilemma of a rising global labor-force coupled with the explosion of automation replacing many jobs. Trials to condense five-days' work into four days focus on productivity: working out how to produce the same amount, to the same quality in less time. This is not about doing things faster, it is about doing things smarter, so that inefficiencies can be removed and innovation deployed. An incentive of an extra day to use as you like is obviously very attractive.

For office-based jobs, it is easy to see how cutting out some of the time spent on nonproductive tasks such as chatting to people and randomly surfing the net could lead to the same amount of work being produced within a shorter space of time. In physical production, it could be more about automating stages. However, the "wasted" time in an office setting is often not really wasted as discussed earlier in this book: it is often spent forming connections. Many jobs that depend on people being available to others, whether in health care or retail for example, can't be condensed without reducing quality, so the outcome might be a rather two-tier system of jobs suitable for a shorter working week versus those that are not. That, of course, would not be fair and if implemented would lead to a lot of guilt for the beneficiaries and potential bitterness (and demands for pay increases) from those locked out of the shorter working week system.

Care is also needed not to move goalposts on productivity to meet new and unsustainable targets. Experiments often yield exaggerated results because of the novelty value, and to maintain a 25 percent increase in productivity might be a stretch long-term and lead to, rather than help with well-being problems. Some employers may seize on any improved productivity figures to set new benchmarks for daily work, regardless of number of days worked.

There will be no rowing back on working arrangements that incorporate at least some remote work, probably an increasing proportion. This leaves organizations with a few practical problems. One of these is whether to maintain prestigious headquarters or downsize to something more humble and perhaps fitting in these uncertain times. Sharp thinking can repurpose surplus buildings into film and photo-shoot locations, general meeting locations for several business who don't have physical space of their own, even sports and social spaces made available generally to staff and their families, wherever their main location. It is this kind of imaginative thinking that will be needed in the future world of work.

Whatever the future holds, remote work will be part of it. We might be looking back in a few years, wondering how anyone put up with going into an office five days a week. We might also be thinking about what to do with our four-day weekend or preparing for our online side-hustle job. The possibilities are numerous and exciting. I look forward to sharing them with you.

Conclusion

Technology and globalization have changed the way the way that we work. We are no longer confined to working from an office, communicating with colleagues and others locally—our closest workmate is now often the technology that we use to collaborate with people around the world. This has massively expanded the potential of what we can do at work and online communication has freed us up to work from anywhere with an Internet connection.

It is not just having the capability but also having the will and the expectation that accompanies mass change in working practices. Social media, with its focus on living in a more flexible and personally oriented way, created the backdrop for many people to decide to prioritize contentment with their work environment over more material issues like pay. Remote work meant that people gained the power to make decisions based on what they wanted to do regarding where they lived and when they worked, as opposed to having to fit these major life decisions to the requirements of employers.

Covid provided the timely and freakish catalyst that changed remote working from a work experiment, alongside things like shorter working weeks and universal basic income, into a legally mandated and global savior of work and economies. Of course, when the mandate for so many people to work at home was lifted, the landscape and people's expectations had changed and things will never be the same again.

Remote work is now a staple of the working environment and, in the guise of hybrid work, the fastest growing working arrangement. With all indicators pointing to the need for organizations to cut costs as economic conditions unwind after many years of quantitative easing and low interest rates, the cost savings of remote work make sense. For many workers, the opportunity to work in a way that gives more flexibility and saves money is now a necessity.

The great remote work surge also uncovered the elephant in the room: people did not need managing in the same way and could be just as productive effectively managing themselves. Covid provided an emperor's new clothes moment revealing that many managers were effectively surplus to requirements and changed power dynamics forever.

Of our time, the remote working models are not without their issues however. In particular, the loneliness epidemic that is also a consequence of most of us living an increasingly individualistic and online-oriented life. Working online through screens does not provide the human contact needed for our mental health and other features of remote work, such as the temptation to work from one online meeting to another, without the informal recuperation time allowed for in offices, can be very negative for well-being and for social development.

The way that remote work is designed and managed therefore is very important. Hybrid working provides an opportunity to bridge the gap between fully remote and on-site work, allowing people to make the connections needed for well-being and for career development. Hybrid working retains the attachments to a physical presence that can be very important in terms of creating organizational culture and group identity. Any form of remote work does however need a new style of management, one that provides the structure needed to keep people organized, while respecting the new balance of power that exists between managers and workers—one that is less based on ego and authority and more based on partnership and trust. This is an emerging area of management science to which this book aims to contribute.

The fast-moving facts on the ground truly make working arrangements one of the most critical issues of our time. People now want freedom to be themselves and have their well-being respected. Employers have an interest in maintaining their labor supply, productivity, and looking after the welfare of their employees. Individual managers and entire organizations are facing challenges over power dynamics and new global trading scenarios. Some business sectors are changing rapidly to accommodate remote working, while others are facing labor shortages as people take decisions to move elsewhere. Some roles are not suitable for remote working at present, while remote working arrangements may lock out people without the facilities to work from home, leaving some people with fewer employment opportunities. All of these issues will likely lead to structural changes in the way that the labor market operates and jobs are priced in future.

At present, remote working is seen as highly desirable by many, but to keep it so, it needs to be well-managed and properly thought out. In particular, the impact of remote working on the psychology of people and their well-being needs considerable research. Remote working should be better understood as the culmination of the biggest changes in work technology and social expectation in modern times. So far, organizations have not fully caught up with the reality of these changes in terms of power dynamics and management practice. I hope to watch the rapid rise of understanding and excellence in the management of remote work.

Bibliography

Bero, T. 2021. "Employees Are Accepting Pay Cuts to Keep Working From Home. They Shouldn't." *The Guardian*. www.theguardian.com/commentisfree/2021 /sep/27/employee-pay-cuts-work-from-home.

Brooks, A.C. 2021. "The Hidden Toll of Remote Work." *The Atlantic*. www .theatlantic.com/family/archive/2021/04/zoom-remote-work-loneliness -happiness/618473/.

Cassidy, F. 2022. *Has Hybrid Working Triggered a Loneliness Epidemic?* Raconteur. www.raconteur.net/healthcare/mental-health/has-hybrid-working-triggered -a-loneliness-epidemic/.

De Smet, A., B. Dowling, M. Mugayar-Baldocchi, and B. Schaninger. 2022. *Gone for Now, or Gone for Good?* McKinsey & Company. www.mckinsey.com /business-functions/people-and-organizational-performance/our-insights /gone-for-now-or-gone-for-good-how-to-play-the-new-talent-game-and -win-back-workers.

Gerdeman, D. 2021. *COVID Killed the Traditional Workplace. What Should Companies Do Now?* Harvard Business School. https://hbswk.hbs.edu/item /covid-killed-the-traditional-workplace-what-should-companies-do-now.

Gitlab. *What Does Hybrid-Remote Mean?* https://about.gitlab.com/company/culture /all-remote/hybrid-remote/.

Goleman, D. 2004. "What Makes a Leader." *Harvard Business Review*. https:// hbr.org/2004/01/what-makes-a-leader.

Holdsworth, L. 2003. "The Psychological Impact of Teleworking: Stress, Emotions and Health." *New Technology, Work and Employment* 18, no. 3. www.thecdi.net /write/Documents/Wales%20Forum/Sandi_Mann_Holdworth.pdf.

Kamal, R. 2022. "Quitting Is Just Half the Story: The Truth Behind the 'Great Resignation'." *The Guardian*. www.theguardian.com/business/2022/jan/04 /great-resignation-quitting-us-unemployment-economy.

Kirby, J. 2021. "Doctors Wanting to Work Part-Time Could Lead to Staff Shortages, College Says." *Evening Standard*. www.standard.co.uk/news/uk /royal-college-of-physicians-doctors-b944091.html.

Klass, P. 2020. "Young Adults' Pandemic Mental Health Risks." *New York Times*. www.nytimes.com/2020/08/24/well/family/young-adults-mental-health -pandemic.html.

Knight, R. 2015. "How to Manage Remote Direct Reports." *Harvard Business Review*. https://hbr.org/2015/02/how-to-manage-remote-direct-reports.

Korolevich, S. 2021. *The State of Remote Work in 2021: A Survey of the American Workforce*. Goodhire. www.goodhire.com/resources/articles/state-of-remote-work-survey/.

Larson, B., S. Vroman, and E. Makarius. 2020. "A Guide to Managing Your (Newly) Remote Workers." *Harvard Business Review*. https://hbr.org/2020/03/a-guide-to-managing-your-newly-remote-workers.

Lilly, C. 2022. *Working From Home (WFH) Statistics*. Finder. www.finder.com/uk/working-from-home-statistics.

Lufkin, B. 2021. *Why Presenteeism Wins Out Over Productivity*. BBC Worklife. www.bbc.com/worklife/article/20210604-why-presenteeism-always-wins-out-over-productivity.

Millet, J. 2021. "How Companies Can Thrive in the Emerging Era of Hybrid Work." *Forbes*. www.forbes.com/sites/forbeshumanresourcescouncil/2021/06/30/how-companies-can-thrive-in-the-emerging-era-of-hybrid-work/?sh=5d14c9326efe.

O'Connor, B. 2021. *The Workers Pushing Back on the Return to the Office*. BBC Worklife. www.bbc.com/worklife/article/20210618-the-workers-pushing-back-on-the-return-to-the-office.

Office for National Statistics. 2021. *Changes in the Economy Since the 1970s*. www.ons.gov.uk/economy/economicoutputandproductivity/output/articles/changesintheeconomysincethe1970s/2019-09-02.

Office for National Statistics. 2022. *Homeworking and Spending During the Coronavirus (COVID-19) Pandemic, Great Britain: April 2020 to January 2022*. www.ons.gov.uk/employmentandlabourmarket/peopleinwork/employmentandemployeetypes/articles/homeworkingandspendingduringthecoronaviruscovid19pandemicgreatbritain/april2020tojanuary2022.

Office for National Statistics. 2022. *Is Hybrid Working Here to Stay?* www.ons.gov.uk/employmentandlabourmarket/peopleinwork/employmentandemployeetypes/articles/ishybridworkingheretostay/2022-05-23.

Oliver, K.H. 2020. *Are You Feeling Zoom-ed Out? You Are not Alone*. Vanderbilt School of Medicine. https://medschool.vanderbilt.edu/basic-sciences/2020/10/01/are-you-feeling-zoom-ed-out-you-are-not-alone/.

Papadatou, A. 2019. *1 of 5 British Children Want a Career as Social Media Influencers*. www.hrreview.co.uk/hr-news/1-of-5-british-children-want-a-career-as-social-media-influencers/114597#:~:text=New%20research%20has%20uncovered%20that,aiming%20to%20become%20a%20YouTuber.

Partridge, J. and P. Inman. 2022. "Hybrid Working Grew in Great Britain Even as Covid Rules Eased, Data Shows." *The Guardian*. www.theguardian.com/business/2022/may/23/hybrid-working-grew-in-great-britain-even-as-covid-rules-eased-data-shows.

Patel, R. 2021. *Remote Working – Let's Not Get Carried Away*. Understanding Society. www.understandingsociety.ac.uk/blog/2021/11/01/remote-working -%E2%80%93-let%E2%80%99s-not-get-carried-away.

Reclaim.ai Blog. 2022. *What Is a Hybrid Work Model? Benefits vs. Challenges.* https://reclaim.ai/blog/what-is-hybrid-work.

Segal, E. 2022. "How Employers Are Enticing Workers Back to the Office." *Forbes.* www.forbes.com/sites/edwardsegal/2022/04/22/how-companies-are-getting -their-employees-to-return-to-the-workplace/?sh=1750cb6a30b1.

Sillars, J. 2021. "COVID-19: People Working From Home in UK More Than Doubled as Pandemic Struck—But at What Cost?" *Sky News.* https://news .sky.com/story/covid-19-8-4-million-were-working-from-home-last-year-as -pandemic-struck-12309068.

Simpson, E. 2022. "The Workers Getting 100% Pay for 80% of the Hours." *BBC News.* www.bbc.co.uk/news/business-61570021.

TUC. 2019. *Annual Commuting Time Is Up 21 Hours Compared to a Decade Ago, Finds TUC.* www.tuc.org.uk/news/annual-commuting-time-21-hours -compared-decade-ago-finds-tuc.

UK Parliament. 2021. *The Impact of Remote and Flexible Working Arrangements.* https://post.parliament.uk/the-impact-of-remote-and-flexible-working -arrangements/.

University of Cambridge. 2022. *Managing Your Team Remotely.* www.hr.admin .cam.ac.uk/files/managing_your_team_remotely.pdf.

Zitron, E. 2021. "Why Managers Fear a Remote-Work Future." *The Atlantic.* www .theatlantic.com/ideas/archive/2021/07/work-from-home-benefits/619597/.

About the Author

Nyla Naseer is a critical thinker in the field of social psychology, economics, and well-being, addressing these complex subjects in a refreshingly down-to-earth and accessible way. An adviser on change, she tackles issues with pragmatism and a deep understanding of how people behave in a fast-changing and ambiguous world. Qualified in management, law, and education, she is a Fellow and previous chair of the RSA in the West Midlands and a Common Purpose Leadership graduate. Based in Birmingham, UK, she works internationally, adding to global discourse by presenting her views in books, articles, and discussions.

Nyla investigates the issues that challenge us today: uncertainty, change, money, power, and well-being. She encourages us to consider how to approach new situations and look again at the way that we handle familiar ones. Challenging stereotypes and testing the untested, she gives voice to alternative perspectives.

A former advocacy specialist, she is not afraid to suggest unconventional solutions based on her observations and research, as opposed to conventional advice and rhetoric. A good example of her original thinking is her work on the power of walking to strengthen problem-solving, creative thinking, and resilience.

Nyla has a BSc in Management Science, a Master of Law degree, specializing in corporate law and an MSc in Urban Regeneration. Away from her work in strategic change and her writing, she can frequently be seen pounding the footpaths as a long-distance hiker.

Other Books by Nyla Naseer

At Walking Pace

At Walking Pace explains why walking is the unsung hero of our times. It helps readers to gain or regain an understanding of the practical benefits of walking to well-being, enjoyment, thinking, and resilience. Walking is the most natural means of getting around under your own steam and the only sustained dynamic exercise that it is possible for nearly all of us to participate in (even if we go slowly at first). No special skills or equipment are required and you can do it anywhere. Walking is flexible enough to be accommodated into occupational and domestic routines, as well as for leisure or specific fitness training. Exploring the evolutionary and historical importance of walking, this book uncovers how the principles that motivated people to walk in the past are even more relevant in the 21st century. Walking can help you get fitter, feel better, and work smarter during these uncertain and hectic times. Life really is better "at walking pace." *At Walking Pace* enlightens you to the ways that walking can enhance your life, whether you want to start walking in earnest for health or well-being reasons, or because you are curious about just how walking can make an impact on your life. Using a combination of research study information, observation, and experience, the author has summarized the ways that you can use walking in your life. The book also delves into the extra elements that can enhance your experience of walking and the benefits that it brings you; for example, does playing music while you walk make a difference, or should you try some problem-solving while you are on the move? The book is packed with information from research, observation, and the personal experience of the author and others. It is a readable, interesting, and useful take on the joy of walking.

Digital Downsize

The undisputed power of digital technology increasingly controls the way that we live—how we communicate, work, and socialize. Alongside the tremendous opportunities that digital technology brings, concerns are growing about problems ranging from cybercrime to behavioral programming, addiction, and isolation. *Digital Downsize* is a wide-ranging introduction to some of these issues. Looking particularly at the impact of social media and other digital communications, it examines topics including

- How psychology and behavior is modified by digital technology.
- The impact on relationships, skills, and social resilience.
- Living and working in an "always-on" environment.

As people's relationship with the online world continues to evolve, and we become increasingly engulfed and mesmerized by its promises, are we using technology wisely—and do we care? This book explores these questions, and looks how young people, in particular, may be affected. *Digital Downsize* promotes a different sort of relationship between people and digital technology: one where people use technology in a more "aware" and balanced way.

It ends by offering practical suggestions for how to optimize the way that digi-tech is used, so that it enhances, rather than detracts from, quality of life. This is an accessible book that should make all of us sit back and think about our present and future relationship with digital technology in a post-COVID-19 world.

Index

OTHER TITLES IN THE HUMAN RESOURCE MANAGEMENT AND ORGANIZATIONAL BEHAVIOR COLLECTION

Michael J. Provitera, Barry University, Editor

- *The Intrapreneurship Formula* by Sandra Lam
- *Navigating Conflict* by Lynne Curry
- *Innovation Soup* by Sanjay Puligadda and Don Waisanen
- *The Aperture for Modern CEOs* by Sylvana Storey
- *The Future of Human Resources* by Tim Baker
- *Change Fatigue Revisited* by Richard Dool and Tahsin I. Alam
- *Championing the Cause of Leadership* by Ted Meyer
- *Embracing Ambiguity* by Michael Edmondson
- *Breaking the Proactive Paradox* by Tim Baker
- *The Modern Trusted Advisor* by Nancy MacKay and Alan Weiss
- *Achieving Success as a 21st Century Manager* by Dean E. Frost
- *A.I. and Remote Working* by Tony Miller
- *Best Boss!* by Duncan Ferguson, Toni M. Pristo, and John Furcon
- *Managing for Accountability* by Lynne Curry
- *Fundamentals of Level Three Leadership* by James G.S. Clawson

Concise and Applied Business Books

The Collection listed above is one of 30 business subject collections that Business Expert Press has grown to make BEP a premiere publisher of print and digital books. Our concise and applied books are for...

- Professionals and Practitioners
- Faculty who adopt our books for courses
- Librarians who know that BEP's Digital Libraries are a unique way to offer students ebooks to download, not restricted with any digital rights management
- Executive Training Course Leaders
- Business Seminar Organizers

Business Expert Press books are for anyone who needs to dig deeper on business ideas, goals, and solutions to everyday problems. Whether one print book, one ebook, or buying a digital library of 110 ebooks, we remain the affordable and smart way to be business smart. For more information, please visit www.businessexpertpress.com, or contact sales@businessexpertpress.com.

9 781637 424599